FINDING LIGHT
IN A DARK WORLD

FINDING LIGHT
IN A DARK WORLD

JAMES E. FAUST

Deseret Book Company
Salt Lake City, Utah

Books by James E. Faust

To Reach Even Unto You
Reach Up for the Light

Library of Congress Cataloging-in-Publication Data

Faust, James E., 1920–
   Finding light in a dark world / James E. Faust.
     p.   cm.
   Includes bibliographical references and index.
   ISBN 1-57345-100-2
   1. Spiritual life—Church of Jesus Christ of Latter-day Saints.
  I. Title.
   BX8656.F376   1995
   248.4'89332—dc20   95-33347
                                                    CIP

Printed in the United States of America

10 9 8 7 6 5 4 3 2 1

To my beloved wife, Ruth,
in appreciation for more than fifty years of loving support.
Her queenly attributes and supernal matriarchal gifts
have brought great joy to me and our family.

Contents

CONTENTS

PART THREE

"BRING UP YOUR CHILDREN IN LIGHT AND TRUTH"
Parents, Priesthood, and Children

Preface

Since becoming a General Authority in 1972, I have had the opportunity to meet with Latter-day Saints in many nations. In doing so, I have seen the countless ways in which faithful members of the Church are working to find light in this ever-darkening world. Good people everywhere are reading the scriptures, studying the gospel, teaching others, and rearing families, often serving without attention or recognition as they brighten the lives of those around them.

In this book—a collection of some of my recent general conference addresses and other speeches edited for the benefit of the reader—I have tried to define the light of the gospel and to suggest some ways in which we might seek that light.

Ancient and modern revelations proclaim Jesus Christ to be the Light of the world. Accordingly, the first section of this book focuses on our need to build stronger testimonies of our Savior, Jesus Christ, "the true Light, which lighteth every man that cometh into the world" (John 1:9).

The second section of the book shows several ways in which we as Latter-day Saints may serve as examples to those around us, thus radiating the light of the gospel: by honoring the legacy of those who have gone before, by performing service and standing for truth in our communities and nations, and by following the example of our Savior in great and small ways.

PREFACE

The concluding section of this book discusses the responsibility of parents to "bring up your children in light and truth . . . , according to the commandments" (D&C 93:40, 42). It is my firm belief that there is no more important human effort. Because each family member has the opportunity to seek the light of the gospel through righteous living, I have devoted specific chapters to discussing the duties and challenges of young people, priesthood holders, mothers, and fathers. And because keeping the Sabbath day holy is a family duty, a chapter addresses that important and sacred topic.

It is hoped that in these pages the reader may find some messages that will strengthen resolve, build testimony, and encourage good works. May the Lord bless you in your efforts to live worthy of his promise: "If your eye be single to my glory, your whole bodies shall be filled with light, and there shall be no darkness in you; and that body which is filled with light comprehendeth all things" (D&C 88:67).

PART ONE

THE LIGHT OF THE WORLD
Jesus Christ, Our Savior

CHAPTER ONE

"The Prints of the Nails in His Hands"

IMAGINE WITH ME that we are going to meet the Savior of the world. Imagine further that we are among the Nephites round about the temple in the land Bountiful on the American continent just after the Savior's crucifixion in Jerusalem. Imagine further that we have received the sign concerning his death, and while we were thus conversing together we "heard a voice as if it came out of heaven" which we could not understand even though "it was not a harsh voice, neither was it a loud voice; nevertheless, . . . it did pierce [us] to the very soul," so much so that there was no part of our bodies that did not quake, causing our "hearts to burn" (3 Nephi 11:3). We heard the voice a second time and we "understood it not" (verse 4).

The third time, we look upward from whence the sound comes. This time we are able to "understand the voice" and it says, "Behold my Beloved Son, in whom I am well pleased, in whom I have glorified my name—hear ye him" (verses 6–7). As we look up, we see "a Man descending out of heaven." He is "clothed in a white robe," and he comes down and stands among us (verse 8). We are frightened. Many of us think it is an angel who has appeared. But he stretches forth his hand and says: "Behold, I am Jesus Christ, whom the prophets testified shall come into the world" (verse 10). He continues: "And behold, I am the light and the life of the world; and I have drunk out of that bitter cup which the Father hath given me, and have glorified the Father in taking upon me the sins of the world, in the which I have suffered the will of the Father in all things from the beginning" (verse 11).

When we hear this, we fall to the earth because we remember that it was prophesied that Christ would show himself unto us after his ascension into heaven. Now we must be sure. There have been many false Christs who have come. How can we know? We remember scriptures that tell the manner of his crucifixion, and he invites us to come forth "that ye may thrust your hands into my side, and also that ye may feel the prints of the nails in my hands and in my feet, that ye may know that I am the God of Israel, and the God of the whole earth, and have been slain for the sins of the world" (verse 14).

At first we are reluctant to do this. It is too personal, too indelicate, to touch another person's body to satisfy our curiosity. Others are getting in line. In the end, our curiosity gets the best of us, because we feel we must know. Is this personage really the Christ, Jesus of Nazareth, who received these marks he offers to show us when he was crucified in Jerusalem?

We are excited. Our hearts pound within our breasts. Could this possibly be the Son of God, the sovereign of the world? The line we are in moves forward, and we walk up to him. As we have been invited to do, we are among those who thrust their hands into his side and feel the prints of the nails in his hands and in his feet. "One by one" we go by him, and then we "know of a surety" that it is he "of whom it was written by the prophets, that should come" (verse 15). All doubt has disappeared.

Having thus witnessed for ourselves, how should we express ourselves? We are so humbled we feel we must say, "Hosanna!" *Hosanna* in the Hebrew means "please save us." And then we say, "Blessed be the name of the Most High God!" and we "fall down at the feet of Jesus, and . . . worship him" (verse 17).

There is one of us in the multitude who is called up to meet the Savior. His name is Nephi. We wonder, how will he greet the Savior? Will he shake hands? Will he bow? What would be appro-

"The Prints of the Nails in His Hands"

priate? We watch very intently. "And Nephi arose and went forth, and bowed himself before the Lord and did kiss his feet" (verse 19). The Lord commands Nephi to arise and gives to him the power to baptize, and he then instructs Nephi and the others to whom he has given the power to baptize how it shall be done. "And now behold, these are the words which ye shall say, calling them by name, saying: Having authority given me of Jesus Christ, I baptize you in the name of the Father, and of the Son, and of the Holy Ghost. Amen" (verses 24–25).

And then we hear the Savior instruct Nephi and the others that following the baptismal prayer, those being baptized should be immersed in the water. We are so anxious to hear more of his message. What will he teach us? He assures us that this is his doctrine and that if we will build upon this, we will build upon a rock, and our lives and our homes will be so strong that "the gates of hell shall not prevail against them" (verse 39). What a great promise that is. We are eager to hear more.

He begins to teach us. We soon hear that the doctrine of Christ is not easy doctrine. We are told we will be judged in part by the intent of our hearts. In large measure, we will be judged not only by what we have done but by what we should have done in a given situation. This is very sobering. It is new to us. This new doctrine requires a reconciliation of differences before we come to the Lord asking his divine providence. "Go thy way unto thy brother, and first be reconciled to thy brother, and then come unto me with full purpose of heart, and I will receive you" (3 Nephi 12:24). Then follows more of the hard doctrine of this Jesus:

> And behold, it is written, an eye for an eye, and a tooth for a tooth;
> But I say unto you, that ye shall not resist evil, but whosoever shall smite thee on thy right cheek, turn to him the other also;
> And if any man will sue thee at the law and take away thy coat, let him have thy cloak also;

And whosoever shall compel thee to go a mile, go with him twain. . . .

And behold it is written also, that thou shalt love thy neighbor and hate thine enemy;

But behold I say unto you, love your enemies, bless them that curse you, do good to them that hate you, and pray for them who despitefully use you and persecute you. (Verses 38–41, 43–44)

At first we are not wise enough to see what the Savior is trying to teach us. Afterward we realize that he is challenging us, trying to raise us to a higher level of devotion.

Now comes the hardest doctrine of all.

"Old things are done away, and all things have become new.

"Therefore I would that ye should be perfect even as I, or your Father who is in heaven is perfect" (verses 47–48).

This is indeed a difficult doctrine. Yet we will try to live it, for our hearts have been changed like those of the Nephites who see the risen Christ and whose descendants for the next two hundred years live in such a manner that there is "no contention in the land, because of the love of God which did dwell in the hearts of the people" (4 Nephi 1:15; see also verse 22).

I close with my own personal testimony. I bear solemn witness that Jesus Christ was born in this life to Mary, having been divinely conceived, and was the very Son of God. I believe that he was indeed born in a manger and reared in the home of Joseph, learning the trade of a carpenter from his stepfather. I believe that he lived among our Heavenly Father's children and taught them the plan of truth and salvation, which, if they are obedient, will permit them to enjoy his eternal presence.

I believe that, having completed his earthly ministry, he worked out our atonement through exquisite personal sacrifice and suffering on his part. I believe that his resurrection was accomplished, that he arose from the tomb with the same form of body parts that he laid down. I believe that he was and is our intercessor

"*The Prints of the Nails in His Hands*"

and advocate with the Father, and that because of him all mankind will enjoy an eternal existence, but that only the obedient and faithful will be exalted in his kingdom.

I believe that in these latter days, through him, a restoration of the holy priesthood after the order of the Son of God, with its keys and authority, has taken place through Joseph Smith. I believe that these same keys and authority have been passed down through the presidents of the Church and are upon the earth, being held at this time by President Gordon B. Hinckley.

I bear solemn testimony that God's purpose for man was declared to Moses: "For behold, this is my work and my glory—to bring to pass the immortality and eternal life of man" (Moses 1:39).

CHAPTER TWO

"A Surety of a Better Testament"

I SHOULD LIKE TO EXAMINE the text of the apostle Paul to the Hebrews: "By so much was Jesus made a surety of a better testament" (Hebrews 7:22). What is a surety? We find in turning to the dictionary that surety is the state of being sure; it is also a pledge given for the fulfillment of an undertaking; it also refers to one who has become legally liable for the debt, default, or failure in duty of another.[1] Does not the Savior, with his mission, have claim upon all these meanings?

What is a testament? To us, the primary meaning of a testament is that it is a covenant with God. It is also holy scripture, a will, a witness, a tangible proof, an expression of conviction.[2] So the Savior as a surety is a guarantor of a better covenant with God.

We all know that moving from the Old Testament to the New Testament is coming from the rigid formality of the letter of the law to the Spirit. The New Testament is a better testament because the intent of a person alone becomes part of the rightness or wrongness of human action. So our intent to do evil or our desire to do good will be a freestanding element of consideration of our actions. We are told we will be judged in part by the intent of our hearts (see D&C 88:109). An example of being convicted by free-standing intent is found in Matthew:

"Ye have heard that it was said by them of old time, Thou shalt not commit adultery:

THE LIGHT OF THE WORLD

"But I say unto you, That whosoever looketh on a woman to lust after her hath committed adultery with her already in his heart" (Matthew 5:27–28).

This New Testament is harder doctrine. A formality and rigidity developed in the administration of the old English common law to the point where, for justice to obtain, the law of equity developed. One of my favorite maxims in equity is "Equity does what ought to be done." The New Testament goes further. In a large measure we will be judged not only by what we have done but what we should have done in a given situation.

Much of the spirit of the New Testament is found in the Sermon on the Mount. The New Testament requires a reconciliation of differences. "Therefore if thou bring thy gift to the altar, and there rememberest that thy brother hath ought against thee;

"Leave there thy gift before the altar, and go thy way; first be reconciled to thy brother, and then come and offer thy gift" (verses 23–24).

Another example of the harder doctrine the Savior taught in the New Testament is this passage, in which swearing becomes completely prohibited:

> Again, ye have heard that it hath been said by them of old time, Thou shalt not forswear thyself, but shalt perform unto the Lord thine oaths:
> But I say unto you, Swear not at all; neither by heaven; for it is God's throne:
> Nor by the earth; for it is his footstool: neither by Jerusalem; for it is the city of the great King.
> Neither shalt thou swear by thy head, because thou canst not make one hair white or black.
> But let your communication be, Yea, yea; Nay, nay: for whatsoever is more than these cometh of evil. (Verses 33–37)

The text that follows is more of the hard doctrine of the New Testament:

"A Surety of a Better Testament"

But I say unto you, That ye resist not evil: but whosoever shall smite thee on thy right cheek, turn to him the other also.

And if any man will sue thee at the law, and take away thy coat, let him have thy cloke also.

And whosoever shall compel thee to go a mile, go with him twain.

Give to him that asketh thee, and from him that would borrow of thee turn not thou away.

Ye have heard that it hath been said, Thou shalt love thy neighbour, and hate thine enemy.

But I say unto you, Love your enemies, bless them that curse you, do good to them that hate you, and pray for them which despitefully use you, and persecute you. (Verses 39–44)

The New Testament suggests a new form and content of prayer. It is profoundly simple and uncomplicated:

And when thou prayest, thou shalt not be as the hypocrites are: for they love to pray standing in the synagogues and in the corners of the streets, that they may be seen of men. Verily I say unto you, They have their reward.

But thou, when thou prayest, enter into thy closet, and when thou hast shut thy door, pray to thy Father which is in secret; and thy Father which seeth in secret shall reward thee openly.

But when ye pray, use not vain repetitions, as the heathen do: for they think that they shall be heard for their much speaking.

Be not ye therefore like unto them: for your Father knoweth what things ye have need of, before ye ask him.

After this manner therefore pray ye: Our Father which art in heaven, Hallowed be thy name.

Thy kingdom come. Thy will be done in earth, as it is in heaven.

Give us this day our daily bread.

And forgive us our debts, as we forgive our debtors.

And lead us not into temptation, but deliver us from evil: For thine is the kingdom, and the power, and the glory, for ever. Amen. (Matthew 6:5–13)

The New Testament suggests that the doing of our good works ought to be in secret:

"But when thou doest alms, let not thy left hand know what thy right hand doeth:

"That thine alms may be in secret: and thy Father which seeth in secret himself shall reward thee openly" (verses 3–4).

But the greatest challenge, the hardest doctrine, is also found in the Sermon on the Mount:

"Be ye therefore perfect, even as your Father which is in heaven is perfect" (Matthew 5:48).

The Savior as "the mediator of the new testament" (Hebrews 9:15) introduces a higher law of marriage:

And the Pharisees came to him, and asked him, Is it lawful for a man to put away his wife? tempting him.

And he answered and said unto them, What did Moses command you?

And they said, Moses suffered to write a bill of divorcement, and to put her away.

And Jesus answered and said unto them, For the hardness of your heart he wrote you this precept.

But from the beginning of the creation God made them male and female.

For this cause shall a man leave his father and mother, and cleave to his wife;

And they twain shall be one flesh: so then they are no more twain, but one flesh.

What therefore God hath joined together, let not man put asunder. (Mark 10:2–9)

The challenge Jesus issued was for people to replace the rigid, technical "thou shalt not" of the law of Moses—needed by the spiritually immature children of Israel—with the spirit of the "better testament." How was this to be done? Time was short. The Savior had only three years. How should he begin? Obviously he must begin with the apostles and the small group of disciples around him who would have the responsibility to carry on the work afterward.

President J. Reuben Clark Jr. describes this challenge as follows: "This task involved the overturning, the virtual outlawing, of the centuries-old Mosaic law of the Jews, and the substitution therefor of the Gospel of Christ."[3]

It was not easy for even the apostles to understand, the doubting Thomas being an example of their lack of comprehension. Thomas had heard the Savior, on several occasions, foretell of his death and resurrection. Yet when Thomas was told that the resurrected Christ lived, he said, "Except I shall see in his hands the print of the nails, and put my finger into the print of the nails, and thrust my hand into his side, I will not believe" (John 20:25). Perhaps Thomas can be forgiven because so great an event had never happened before.

What about Peter's conversion to the great principle that the gospel of Jesus Christ is for everyone? He had been an eyewitness, as he stated in 2 Peter: "For we have not followed cunningly devised fables, when we made known unto you the power and coming of our Lord Jesus Christ, but were eyewitnesses of his majesty" (2 Peter 1:16). To what had he been an eyewitness? He had been an eyewitness to everything in the Savior's ministry. Following Christ's encounter with the Samaritan at the well of Jacob, Peter had seen the Savior welcome the Samaritans, who were loathed by the Jews (see John 4). Peter had seen a vision and heard the voice of the Lord, saying, "What God hath cleansed, that call not thou common" (Acts 10:15). Finally, when Peter was fully converted and had received a spiritual confirmation, it is stated that he "opened his mouth, and said, Of a truth I perceive that God is no respecter of persons:

"But in every nation he that feareth him, and worketh righteousness, is accepted with him" (verses 34–35).

It is so strengthening to review the testimonies of the apostles that Jesus is, in fact, the Christ. These testimonies are also a surety of a better testament. The first recorded testimony of the divinity of the Savior is the occasion on which Jesus walked on the water, which is more fully recorded in Matthew 14:

> But the ship was now in the midst of the sea, tossed with waves: for the wind was contrary.
>
> And in the fourth watch of the night Jesus went unto them, walking on the sea.
>
> And when the disciples saw him walking on the sea, they were troubled, saying, It is a spirit; and they cried out for fear.
>
> But straightway Jesus spake unto them, saying, Be of good cheer; it is I; be not afraid.
>
> And Peter answered him and said, Lord, if it be thou, bid me come unto thee on the water.
>
> And he said, Come. And when Peter was come down out of the ship, he walked on the water, to go to Jesus.
>
> But when he saw the wind boisterous, he was afraid; and beginning to sink, he cried, saying, Lord, save me.
>
> And immediately Jesus stretched forth his hand, and caught him, and said unto him, O thou of little faith, wherefore didst thou doubt?
>
> And when they were come into the ship, the wind ceased.
>
> Then they that were in the ship came and worshipped him, saying, Of a truth thou art the Son of God. (Matthew 14:24–33)

The second testimony of the Savior's divinity is that of Peter. The fullest account appears in Matthew, with which we are all familiar:

> And Simon Peter answered and said, Thou art the Christ, the Son of the living God.
>
> And Jesus answered and said unto him, Blessed art thou,

"A Surety of a Better Testament"

> Simon Bar-jona: for flesh and blood hath not revealed it unto thee, but my Father which is in heaven.
>
> And I say also unto thee, That thou art Peter, and upon this rock I will build my church; and the gates of hell shall not prevail against it. (Matthew 16:16–18)

The third recorded instance again involves Peter. Following the great "bread of life" sermon, in which the Savior had made clear to those who had been fed by the loaves and the fishes that he and his doctrine was the bread of life, John records:

> From that time many of his disciples went back, and walked no more with him.
>
> Then said Jesus unto the twelve, Will ye also go away?
>
> Then Simon Peter answered him, Lord, to whom shall we go? thou hast the words of eternal life.
>
> And we believe and are sure that thou art that Christ, the Son of the living God. (John 6:66–69)

The testimony of the divinity of the Savior given by God the Father and heard by Peter, James, and John is recorded in connection with the happenings on the Mount of Transfiguration. The accounts of Matthew, Mark, and Luke all tell of the appearance of Moses and Elias talking to the Savior. Then Matthew records:

> Then answered Peter, and said unto Jesus, Lord, it is good for us to be here: if thou wilt, let us make here three tabernacles; one for thee, and one for Moses, and one for Elias.
>
> While he yet spake, behold, a bright cloud overshadowed them: and behold a voice out of the cloud, which said, This is my beloved Son, in whom I am well pleased; hear ye him.
>
> And when the disciples heard it, they fell on their face, and were sore afraid.
>
> And Jesus came and touched them, and said, Arise, and be not afraid.
>
> And when they had lifted up their eyes, they saw no man, save Jesus only.

THE LIGHT OF THE WORLD

And as they came down from the mountain, Jesus charged them, saying, Tell the vision to no man, until the Son of man be risen again from the dead.

And his disciples asked him, saying, Why then say the scribes that Elias must first come?

And Jesus answered and said unto them, Elias truly shall first come, and restore all things.

But I say unto you, That Elias is come already, and they knew him not, but have done unto him whatsoever they listed. Likewise shall also the Son of man suffer of them.

Then the disciples understood that he spake unto them of John the Baptist. (Matthew 17:4–13)

We are grateful for these profound statements of the "eyewitnesses of his majesty." They form part of the footings of our faith. But the miracles performed by the Savior and the testimonies of those who saw and heard were far from convincing to everyone. This is perhaps because a personal testimony is such a personal, spiritual conviction.

The New Testament is a better testament because so much is left to the intent of the heart and of the mind. This refinement of the soul is part of the reinforcing steel of a personal testimony. If there is no witness in the heart and in the mind, there can be no testimony. Let us study, learn, and live the hard doctrines the Savior taught, that our Christlike behavior may move us up to a much higher spiritual attainment.

NOTES

1. See *Merriam Webster's Collegiate Dictionary*, 10th ed. (Springfield, Mass.: Merriam-Webster, Inc., 1993), p. 1185.

2. *Merriam Webster's Collegiate Dictionary*, 10th ed., p. 1218.

3. *Why the King James Version* (Salt Lake City: Deseret Book Co., 1956), p. 51.

CHAPTER THREE

A Crown of Thorns, a Crown of Glory

LIFE PRESENTS EACH OF US with challenges that eat at us like thorns, briars, and slivers. Our Savior suffered as he wore a crown of thorns. And yet there is also exquisite beauty and fragrance to be found in life, and the potential of receiving a crown of glory. I wish that I better understood all of the divine purposes in having to contend with so many painful irritants in this life. Lehi explained one reason: that we will appreciate and savor the goodness and loveliness of the world (see 2 Nephi 2:10–13). Adam was told that the ground is cursed with thorns and thistles for our sakes (see Genesis 3:17–18). Likewise, mortality is "cursed" with the thorns of worldly temptation and the slivers of sin so that we can be tested and prove ourselves. This is necessary for our eternal progression. The apostle Paul explained, "Lest I should be exalted above measure . . . , there was given to me a thorn in the flesh" (2 Corinthians 12:7).

The denial of our own sins, of our own selfishness, of our own weakness is like a crown of thorns that keeps us from moving up one more step in personal growth. Perhaps worse than sin is the denial of sin. If we deny that we are sinners, how can we ever be forgiven? How can the atonement of Jesus work in our lives if there is no repentance? If we do not promptly remove the slivers of sin and the thorns of carnal temptation, how can the Lord ever heal our souls? The Savior said, "Repent of your sins, and be converted, that I may heal you" (3 Nephi 9:13). It is most difficult for us to pray for those who hate us, who despitefully use us, who persecute us. By failing to take this vital extra step, however, we fail to remove some of the festering briars in our souls. Extending forgiveness, love, and understanding for perceived shortcomings and weaknesses in our wives, husbands, children, and associates makes it much easier to say, "God be merciful to me a sinner" (Luke 18:13).

It seems that no matter how carefully we walk through life's paths, we pick up some thorns, briars, and slivers. When I was a young boy, when school was out for the summer and we went to the farm, off came our shoes. The shoes stayed off all summer long except for special occasions. For the first week or two, when our feet were tender, the smoothest pebble or stick would be painful. But as the weeks came and went, the soles of our feet toughened so that they could withstand almost anything in the path except thistles, of which there seemed to be more than any other weed. And so it is with life: as we grow and mature and keep close to him who was crowned with thorns, our souls seem to get stronger in withstanding the challenges, our resolve hardens, our wills become firmer, and our self-discipline increases to protect us from the evils of this world. These evils are so omnipresent, however, that we must always walk in the paths that are the most free of the thistles of earthly temptation.

As children we used to delight in waving thistledown stalks to watch the seeds float on the wind. Only later did we realize the effects that this had on our own and neighboring gardens. Many of us delight in flirting with temptation, only later to learn how we and others have sown the seeds of our own unhappiness and how we can also affect our neighbor's happiness.

There is a defense mechanism to discern between good and evil. It is called conscience. It is our spirit's natural response to the pain of sin, just like pain in our flesh is our body's natural response to a wound—even a small sliver. Conscience strengthens through use. Paul told the Hebrews, "But strong meat belongeth to them that are of full age, even those who by reason of use have their senses exercised to discern both good and evil" (Hebrews 5:14). Those who have not exercised their conscience have "their conscience seared with a hot iron" (1 Timothy 4:2). A sensitive conscience is a sign of a healthy spirit.

How are the thorns and slivers of life removed? The power to remove the thorns in our lives and in the lives of others begins with ourselves. Moroni writes that when we deny ourselves of ungodliness, then the grace of Christ is sufficient for us (see Moroni 10:32).

Too often we seek bandages to cover the guilt rather than removing the thorn that causes the pain. How much we resist the momentary pain of removing a sliver even though it will relieve the longer-lasting pain of a festering sore. Everyone knows that if thorns and briars and slivers are not removed from the flesh, they will cause sores that fester and will not heal.

One of the members of our family has a remarkable dog named Ben. A few years ago, on a beautiful fall day, some of us were walking in the fields. Ben, his tail wagging, was going back and forth in front of us, sniffing the ground and obviously enjoying himself. After a while we sat down on a ditch bank to rest and could feel the warmth of the autumn sun caressing us. Ben came limping up to his master and, with a pained look in his eye, held up his front paw. Ben's master gently took his paw into his hands and examined it carefully. Between two of his toes was a thorn. The thorn was carefully removed, and Ben stayed long enough to wag his tail a little more vigorously and receive a few pats on his head. He then ran off, no longer limping nor bothered by the pain. I was amazed that Ben instinctively seemed to know that the thorn needed to come out to relieve the pain and to know where to go to have it removed. Like Ben, we also seem to instinctively look for relief from the thorns of sin that inflict us. In contrast, however, we do not always seek our Master for relief; and many do not yet know who their Master is.

As a carpenter, Jesus would have been familiar with slivers and thorny woods. As a child he would have learned that one rarely gets a sliver when working the wood in the right direction. He would also have known more than any how slivers—small and painful—divert attention from important matters. The scourging of Jesus took place partly with thorns:

> Then the soldiers of the governor took Jesus into the common hall, and gathered unto him the whole band of soldiers.
> And they stripped him, and put on him a scarlet robe.
> And when they had platted a crown of thorns, they put it upon his head, and a reed in his right hand: and they bowed the knee before him, and mocked him, saying, Hail, King of the Jews!
> And they spit upon him, and took the reed, and smote him on the head. (Matthew 27:27–30)

Perhaps this cruel act was a perverse attempt to mimic the placing of an emperor's laurel upon his head. Thus, there was pressed down upon him a crown of thorns. He accepted the pain as part of the great gift he had promised to make. How poignant this was, considering that thorns signified God's displeasure as he cursed the ground for Adam's sake that henceforth it would bring forth thorns. But by wearing the crown, Jesus transformed thorns into a symbol of his glory. As Emily Dickinson so aptly described it:

> One crown that no one seeks
> And yet the highest head
> Its isolation coveted
> Its stigma deified.[1]

Because he was focused on giving, neither the adulation nor the scorn of the world could deflect him from his mission.

Our Savior knows "according to the flesh" every dimension of our suffering. There is no infirmity he is not familiar with. In his agony he became acquainted with all of the thorns, slivers, and thistles that might afflict us:

> And he shall go forth, suffering pains and afflictions and temptations of every kind; and this that the word might be

A Crown of Thorns, a Crown of Glory

fulfilled which saith he will take upon him the pains and the sicknesses of his people.

And he will take upon him death, that he may loose the bands of death which bind his people; and he will take upon him their infirmities, that his bowels may be filled with mercy, according to the flesh, that he may know according to the flesh how to succor his people according to their infirmities. (Alma 7:11–12)

All irritants of the flesh and the soul should be removed before they fester. However, though they ulcerate and though they torment, they can still be removed, and the healing process will take place. When the infection is healed, the soreness will leave. That process is known as repentance. Repentance and forgiveness are among the greatest fruits of the Atonement. It is not easy to remove the thorns of pride, the thistles of selfishness, the slivers of ego, and the briars of appetite.

In Roselandia, Brazil, outside the great city of São Paulo, there are many acres of beautiful roses. When one stands on a small hill above the rose fields, the aroma is delightful and the beauty is exhilarating. The thorns on the bushes are there, but they in no way lessen the enjoyment of the sight and the smell. I would challenge all to put the thorns, slivers, and thistles we encounter in life in proper perspective. We should deal with them but then concentrate on the flowers of life, not on the thorns. We should savor the smell and beauty of the flower of the rose and the cactus. To savor the sweet aroma of the blossoms, we need to live righteous and disciplined lives in which the study of the scriptures, prayer, right priorities, and right attitudes are integrated into our lives. For members of this church, that focus sharpens inside our temples. We will all surely encounter some of the thorns, but they are only incidental to the sweet fragrances and exquisite beauty of the blooms. Did not the Savior say: "Ye shall know them by their fruits. Do men gather grapes of thorns, or figs of thistles?" (Matthew 7:16.)

Thomas Carlyle, a British writer, stated, "Every noble crown is, and on Earth will forever be, a crown of thorns."[2] The ancient Latin phrase *sic transit gloria mundi* means "thus passes away the glory of this world." Earthly rewards can be a sore temptation. In contrast, those who are faithful and are committed to service are promised that they will be "crowned with honor, and glory, and immortality, and eternal life" (D&C 75:5). Thus, neither honors nor trials can defeat. Paul spoke of an incorruptible crown (see 1 Corinthians 9:25), and James spoke of the faithful receiving a "crown of life" (James 1:12). John the Revelator counseled, "Hold that fast which thou hast, that no man take thy crown" (Revelation 3:11).

I believe that earthly crowns such as power, the love of money, and the preoccupation with material things and the honors of men are a crown of thorns because they are based upon obtaining and receiving rather than giving. So selfishness can make what we think is a noble crown into a crown of thorns beyond our power to endure. When I first started my professional career, one of the senior members in our office asked another senior member for some help on a legal matter. The other man who was asked to help was gifted and able but also selfish. He replied, "What's in it for me?" The "what's in it for me" philosophy is basically what's wrong with the world. It is surely one of the sharpest points in a crown of thorns.

The call of Jesus Christ to each of us is "If any man will come after me, let him deny himself, and take up his cross, and follow me" (Matthew 16:24). Is it not time that we begin denying ourselves, as the Savior counseled, and surrender and master ourselves rather than indulge ourselves in a selfish, "do my own thing" little world? The question is not so much what we can do but what God can do through us. The apostle Paul said, "If a man therefore purge himself . . . , he shall be a vessel unto honour, sanctified, and meet for the master's use, and prepared unto every good work" (2 Timothy 2:21).

Taking up one's cross and following the Savior is always a

A Crown of Thorns, a Crown of Glory

commitment to service. When going to school I was very poor. I worked long hours in a canning factory catching steaming-hot cans for twenty-five cents an hour. I learned that selfishness has more to do with how we feel about what we have than how much we have. A poor man can be selfish and a rich man generous, but a person obsessed only with getting will have a hard time finding God. I have come to know that with any privilege comes responsibility. Most privilege carries with it the responsibility to serve, to give, and to bless. God can take away any privilege if it is not used under his omnipotent will. Meeting that challenge to give, to serve, to bless in faithfulness and devotion is the only way to enjoy the crown of glory spoken of by the original apostles. It is the only way true meaning comes to life. We will be able to receive honors or scorn with equal serenity.

I conclude with the words of Ezekiel: "And thou, son of man, . . . though briers and thorns be with thee, and thou dost dwell among scorpions: be not afraid" (Ezekiel 2:6). In our constantly changing world, may we continually cling to those things that do not change: to prayer, to faith, to saving covenants, to love of families, and to brotherhood. By removing the slivers of sin and the thorns of worldly temptation in our lives, and by denying ourselves and taking up our own cross and following the Savior, we can change a crown of thorns to a crown of glory. I testify, as one of his humble servants called to be his special witness, that he lives. I witness from the depths of my soul that we are engaged in his holy work, to which, if we are faithful, we can be crowned with honor, glory, and eternal life (see D&C 75:5).

NOTES

1. *The Complete Poems of Emily Dickinson,* ed. Thomas H. Johnson (Boston: Little, Brown and Co., 1960), pp. 703–4.

2. *Past and Present* (London: J. M. Dent and Sons, 1912), 3:173.

CHAPTER FOUR

"He Healeth the Broken in Heart"

IT IS AN INEVITABLE fact of life that from time to time each of us suffers some of the troubles, challenges, and disappointments of this world. When we face the challenges of mortality, we wish there was a sure cure for heartache, disappointment, torment, anguish, and despair. The Psalmist stated, "He healeth the broken in heart, and bindeth up their wounds" (Psalm 147:3). The healing is a divine miracle; the wounds are a common lot of all mankind.

In today's overloaded society, some of the healing agents that our parents enjoyed seem not to be at work in our lives. Fewer and fewer are able to relieve stress by working with their hands and by tilling the soil. The increasing demands, the diversity of voices, the entreating sales pitches, the piercing noises, the entanglement of many personal relationships can rob our souls of the peace they need to function and survive. Our hurry to meet the relentless demands of the clock tears away at our inner peace. The pressures to compete and survive are great. Our appetite for personal possessions seems enormous. The increasing forces that destroy the individual and the family bring great sadness and heartbreak.

One reason for the spiritual sickness of our society is that so many do not know or care about what is morally right and wrong. So many things are justified on the basis of expediency and the acquiring of money and goods. In recent times, those individuals and institutions that have had the courage to stand up and speak out against adultery, dishonesty, violence, gambling, and other forms of evil are often held up to ridicule. Many things are just plainly and simply wrong, whether they are illegal or not. Those who persist in following after the evil things of the world cannot know the "peace of God, which passeth all understanding" (Philippians 4:7).

Someway, somehow, we must find the healing influence that brings solace to the soul. Where is this balm? Where is the compensating relief so desperately needed to help us survive in the world's pressures? The onsetting comfort in large measure can come through increased communion with the Spirit of God. This can bring spiritual healing.

Spiritual healing is illustrated in the story of Warren M. Johnson, pioneer ferryman at Lee's Ferry, Arizona. As a young man, Warren Johnson came west seeking his fortune in gold in the summer of 1866. He became very ill, and his companions left him under a tree in the yard of a family in Bountiful. One of the daughters found him and reported that there was a dead man out in the yard. Although he was a complete stranger, this kind family took him in and nursed him back to health. They taught him the gospel, and he was baptized. He eventually ended up as the ferryman at Lee's Ferry.

In 1891 the Warren Johnson family suffered a great tragedy. Within a short time, they lost four children to diphtheria. All four were buried in a row next to each other. In a letter to President Wilford Woodruff, dated July 29, 1891, Warren told the story:

Dear Brother . . .

In May 1891 a family residing in Tuba City, came here from Richfield Utah, where they . . . spent the winter visiting friends. At Panguitch they buried a child, . . . without disinfecting the wagon or themselves, [and] not even stopping to wash the dead child's clothes, they came to our house, and remained overnight, mingling with my little children. . . .

"He Healeth the Broken in Heart"

We knew nothing of the nature of the disease, but had faith in God, as we were here on a very hard mission, and had tried as hard as we knew how to obey the word of Wisdom, [to] attend to the other duties of our religion, such as paying [our] tithing, family prayers, etc. etc. that our children would be spared. But alas, in four and a half days [the oldest boy] choked to death in my arms. Two more were taken down with the disease and we fasted and prayed as much as we thought it wisdom as we had many duties to perform here. We fasted [for] twenty-four hours and once I fasted [for] forty hours, but to no avail for both my little girls died also. About a week after their death my fifteen year old daughter Melinda was [also] stricken down and we did all we could for her but she [soon] followed the others. . . . Three of my dear girls and one boy [have] been taken from us, and the end is not yet. My oldest girl nineteen years old is now prostrate [from] the disease, and we are fasting and praying in her behalf today. . . . I would ask for your faith and prayers in our behalf however. What have we done that the Lord has left us, and what can we do to gain his favor again[?]

Yours in the gospel

Warren M. Johnson[1]

In a subsequent letter dated August 16, 1891, to his friend Warren Foote, Brother Johnson testified that he had found a spiritual peace:

I can assure you, however, that it is the hardest trial of my life, but I set out for salvation and am determined that . . . through the help of Heavenly Father that I [would] hold fast to the iron rod no matter what troubles [came] upon me. I have not slackened in the performance of my duties, and hope and trust that I shall have the faith and prayers of my brethren, that I can live so as to receive the blessings you having authority . . . placed on my head.[2]

The sixth article of faith states that, among other spiritual gifts, we believe in the gift of healing. To me, this gift extends to the healing of both the body and the spirit. The Spirit speaks peace to the soul. This spiritual solace comes by invoking spiritual gifts, which are claimed and manifested in many ways. They are rich and full and abundant in the Church today. They flow from the proper and humble use of a testimony. They also come through the administering to the sick following an anointing with consecrated oil. Christ is the great Physician, who rose from the dead "with healing in his wings" (2 Nephi 25:13), while the Comforter is the agency of healing.

The Lord has provided many avenues by which we may receive this healing influence. I am grateful that the Lord has restored temple work to the earth. It is an important part of the work of salvation for both the living and the dead. Our temples provide a sanctuary where we may go to lay aside many of the anxieties of the world. Our temples are places of peace and tranquillity. In these hallowed sanctuaries God "healeth the broken in heart, and bindeth up their wounds" (Psalm 147:3).

The reading and the study of the scriptures can bring great comfort. Elder Marion G. Romney, while serving as a member of the Quorum of the Twelve, stated:

> I feel certain that if, in our homes, parents will read from the Book of Mormon prayerfully and regularly, both by themselves and with their children, the spirit of that great book will come to permeate our homes and all who dwell therein. The spirit of reverence will increase, mutual respect and consideration for each other will grow. The spirit of contention will depart. Parents will counsel their children in greater love and wisdom. Children will be more responsive and submissive to that counsel. Righteousness will increase. Faith, hope, and charity—the pure love of Christ—will abound in our homes and lives, bringing in their wake peace, joy, and happiness.[3]

"He Healeth the Broken in Heart"

When I was young, the health benefits of the Word of Wisdom, including abstinence from tobacco, alcoholic drinks, tea, and coffee, were not as well established as they are today. However, the spiritual benefits have long been validated. The Word of Wisdom promises that those who remember to keep this counsel and walk in obedience to the commandments "shall receive health in their navel and marrow to their bones" (D&C 89:18).

Marrow has long been a symbol of vibrant, healthful living. But in a day of lifesaving bone marrow transplants, the phrase "marrow to their bones" takes on an additional significance as a spiritual covenant. The promises for those who keep the Word of Wisdom continue. Those who observe this law "shall find wisdom and great treasures of knowledge, even hidden treasures; and shall run and not be weary, and shall walk and not faint. And I, the Lord, give unto them a promise, that the destroying angel shall pass by them, as the children of Israel, and not slay them" (D&C 89:19–21).

If we are to be spared, we do indeed need to be fortified against the many destroying agents at work in the world today.

However, for many of us, the spiritual healing takes place not in great arenas of the world but in our own sacrament meetings. It is comforting to worship with, partake of the sacrament with, and be taught in a spirit of humility by neighbors and close friends who love the Lord and try to keep his commandments. Our good bishop assigns the participants to treat a gospel subject or principle. Invariably they speak by the power of the Holy Ghost, opening their hearts so that the audience can behold the jewels therein. The messages are given in humble witness and sweet counsel. We of the audience understand that which is taught by the Spirit of truth and verify the accompanying testimonies.

Our sacrament meetings should be worshipful and healing, restoring those who attend to spiritual soundness. Part of this healing process occurs as we worship through music and song. Singing our beautiful, worshipful hymns is food for our souls. We become of one heart and one mind when we sing praises to the Lord.

Among other influences, worshiping in song has the effect of spiritually unifying the participants in an attitude of reverence.

Spiritual healing also comes from bearing and hearing humble testimonies. A witness given in a spirit of contrition, thankfulness for divine providence, and submission to divine guidance is a powerful remedy to relieve the anguish and concerns of our hearts.

I doubt that sincere members of this church can achieve complete spiritual healing without being in harmony with the foundation of the Church, which, the apostle Paul stated, is "the apostles and prophets" (Ephesians 2:20). This may not be the popular thing to do based upon the long history of rejection by the world of the prophets and their messages. Nevertheless, prophets are the oracles of God on earth and those called to lead and direct the work in this day and time. It is also essential for us to be found sustaining our bishops and our stake presidents and other leaders.

Recent information seems to confirm that the ultimate spiritual healing comes in the forgetting of self. A review of the accounts I have read indicates that those who survived best in prison and hostage camps were those who were concerned for their fellow prisoners and were willing to give away their own food and substance to help sustain the others. Dr. Viktor Frankl stated:

> We who lived in concentration camps can remember the men who walked through the huts comforting others, giving away their last piece of bread. They may have been few in number, but they offer sufficient proof that everything can be taken from a man but one thing: the last of . . . human freedoms—to choose one's attitude in any given set of circumstances, [and] to choose one's own way [of life].[4]

The Savior of the world said it very simply: "And whosoever shall lose his life shall preserve it" (Luke 17:33).

Of all that we might do to find solace, prayer is perhaps the most comforting. We are instructed to pray to the Father in the name of his Son, the Lord Jesus Christ, by the power of the Holy Ghost. The very act of praying to God is satisfying to the soul, even though God, in his wisdom, may not give what we ask for. President Harold B. Lee taught us that all of our prayers are answered, but sometimes the Lord says no. The Prophet Joseph Smith taught that the "best way to obtain truth and wisdom" is "to go to God in prayer."[5] Prayer is most helpful in the healing process.

Wounds inflicted by others are healed by the "art of healing." President Joseph F. Smith stated, "But the healing of a wound is an art not acquired by practice alone, but by the loving tenderness that comes from universal good will and a sympathetic interest in the welfare and happiness of others."[6]

There is hope for all to be healed through repentance and obedience. The Prophet Isaiah verified that "though your sins be as scarlet, they shall be as white as snow" (Isaiah 1:18). The Prophet Joseph Smith stated: "There is never a time when the spirit is too old to approach God. All are [in] reach of pardoning mercy."[7]

After our full repentance, the formula is wonderfully simple. Indeed, the Lord has given it to us in these words: "Will ye not now return unto me, and repent of your sins, and be converted, that I may heal you?" (3 Nephi 9:13). In so doing, we have his promise that "he healeth the broken in heart, and bindeth up their wounds" (Psalm 147:3).

We find solace in Christ through the agency of the Comforter, and Christ extends this invitation to us: "Come unto me, all ye that labour and are heavy laden, and I will give you rest" (Matthew 11:28). The apostle Peter speaks of "casting all your care upon him; for he careth for you" (1 Peter 5:7). As we do this, healing takes place, just as the Lord promised through the prophet Jeremiah when he said, "I will turn their mourning into joy, and will comfort them, and make them rejoice from their sorrow. . . . I have satiated the weary soul, and I have replenished every sorrowful soul" (Jeremiah 31:13, 25).

In the celestial glory, we are told, "God shall wipe away all tears from their eyes; and there shall be no more death, neither sorrow, nor crying, neither shall there be any more pain" (Revelation 21:4).

Then faith and hope will replace heartache, disappointment, torment, anguish, and despair, and the Lord will give us strength, as Alma says, that we "should suffer no manner of afflictions, save it were swallowed up in the joy of Christ" (Alma 31:38). May we live to be worthy of that glorious day of rejoicing.

NOTES

1. P. T. Riely, "Warren Marshall Johnson, Forgotten Saint," *Utah Historical Quarterly,* Winter 1971, p. 19; spelling modernized.

2. "Autobiography of Warren Foote of Glendale, Kane County, Utah," LDS Church Archives, Salt Lake City, Utah.

3. In Conference Report, April 1960, pp. 112–13.

4. *Man's Search for Meaning* (New York: Simon and Schuster, 1963), p. 104.

5. *Teachings of the Prophet Joseph Smith,* sel. Joseph Fielding Smith (Salt Lake City: Deseret Book Co., 1938), p. 191.

6. Joseph F. Smith, *Gospel Doctrine,* 5th ed. (Salt Lake City: Deseret Book Co., 1939), p. 264.

7. *Teachings of the Prophet Joseph Smith,* p. 191.

CHAPTER FIVE

Children of Christ,
Heirs to the Kingdom of God

SINCE THE EARLY DAYS of the Church, the General Authorities and missionaries have traveled over much of the earth to proclaim the gospel of Jesus Christ, as restored by the Prophet Joseph Smith, and to establish the Church with keys and authority in many lands. An impressive and enjoyable part of our ministry has been to worship with the wonderful people of many cultures and ethnic groups. It has been soul satisfying to feel of their spiritual strength and their love and to love them in return.

Now the curtains are opening up to more and more of the nonindustrialized nations. In some of these countries, a large percentage of the population is poor. Many of them have much less opportunity than others to acquire the comforts of life and even some of the necessities. We have seen men and women working to exhaustion from sunrise to sundown for a pittance. Yet their ready smiles and cheerful countenances indicated that they had found some happiness with their lot in life.

Some might say, "Where is the justice in the fact that some of God's children have so much of health and this world's goods and others so very little?" So many of those who have in abundance seem unappreciative of what they have. But we have also seen the generosity of members of this church who have great concern for those worldwide who lack the necessities of life. They generously contribute to help the poor in many countries, even though we have no members there. Humanitarian help has been given in 114 countries since 1985.[1]

I have learned to admire, respect, and love the good people from every race, culture, and nation that I have been privileged to visit. In my experience, no race or class seems superior to any other in spirituality and faithfulness. Those who seem less caring spiritually are those individuals—regardless of race, culture, or nationality—spoken of by the Savior in the parable of the sower, individuals who are "choked with cares and riches and pleasures of this life, and bring no fruit to perfection" (Luke 8:14).

One of this nation's leading pollsters, Richard Wirthlin, has identified through polls an expression of the basic needs of people in the United States. These needs are self-esteem, peace of mind, and personal contentment. I believe these are needs of God's children everywhere. How can these needs be satisfied? I suggest that behind each of these is the requirement to establish one's own personal identity as the offspring of God. Regardless of our ethnic background, culture, or country, all three needs can be met if we look to the divinity that is within us. As the Savior himself has said, "The Spirit giveth light to every man [and woman] that cometh into the world; and the Spirit enlighteneth every man [and woman] through the world, that hearkeneth to the voice of the Spirit" (D&C 84:46).

President David O. McKay said:

> Generally there is in man a divinity which strives to push him onward and upward. We believe that this power within him is the spirit that comes from God. Man lived before he came to this earth, and he is here now to strive to perfect the spirit within. At some time in his life, every man is conscious of a desire to come in touch with the Infinite. His spirit reaches out for God. This sense of feeling is universal, and all men ought to be, in deepest truth, engaged in the same great work—the search for and the development of spiritual peace and freedom.[2]

Children of Christ, Heirs to the Kingdom of God

As the humble servants of God—the General Authorities, the missionaries, and others—travel throughout the world, we are compelled to ask: What can we do for the peoples of the earth? What can we give that no one else can? What can justify the great expenditure of effort, time, and means to "go . . . into all the world" (Mark 16:15), as the Savior commanded. We cannot change the economy of countries. We do not seek to change governments. The answer is simple. We can offer the hope promised by the Savior: "Peace in this world, and eternal life in the world to come" (D&C 59:23). Lives are changed as the servants of God teach God's children everywhere to accept and keep the commandments of God. Anyone, regardless of culture or economic circumstance, can go to the depths of his spiritual wells and drink of that water. He that partakes of this water, as the Savior said, "shall never thirst; but the water . . . shall be in him a well of water springing up into everlasting life" (John 4:14). The basic needs of mankind identified by Dr. Wirthlin—self-esteem, peace of mind, and personal contentment—can be fully satisfied by faithful obedience to the commandments of God. This is true of any person in any country or culture.

Though many lack the necessities of life, I take comfort in the words of Nephi: "But they were . . . one, the children of Christ, and heirs to the kingdom of God" (4 Nephi 1:17).

As we move into more and more countries in the world, we find a rich cultural diversity in the Church. Yet everywhere there can be a "unity of the faith" (Ephesians 4:13). Each group brings special gifts and talents to the table of the Lord. We can all learn much of value from each other. But each of us should also voluntarily seek to enjoy all of the unifying and saving covenants, ordinances, and doctrines of the gospel of the Lord Jesus Christ.

In the great diversity of peoples, cultures, and circumstances, we remember that all are equal before the Lord, for as Paul taught:

> Ye are all the children of God by faith in Christ Jesus.
> For as many of you as have been baptized into Christ have put on Christ.

THE LIGHT OF THE WORLD

> There is neither Jew nor Greek, there is neither bond nor free, there is neither male nor female: for ye are all one in Christ Jesus.
>
> And if ye be Christ's, then are ye Abraham's seed, and heirs according to the promise. (Galatians 3:26–29)

We do not lose our identity in becoming members of this church. We become heirs to the kingdom of God, having joined the body of Christ and spiritually set aside some of our personal differences to unite in a greater spiritual cause. We say to all who have joined the Church, keep all that is noble, good, and uplifting in your culture and personal identity. However, under the authority and power of the keys of the priesthood, all differences yield as we seek to become heirs to the kingdom of God, unite in following those who have the keys of the priesthood, and seek the divinity within us. All are welcomed and appreciated. But there is only one celestial kingdom of God.

Our real strength is not so much in our diversity but in our spiritual and doctrinal unity. For instance, the baptismal prayer and baptism by immersion in water are the same all over the world. The sacramental prayers are the same everywhere. We sing the same hymns in praise to God in every country.

The high moral standards of this church apply to all members in every country. Honesty and integrity are taught and expected everywhere. Chastity before marriage and absolute fidelity to wife or husband after marriage are required of members of the Church everywhere. Members who violate these high standards of moral conduct place their Church membership in question anywhere in the world.

The requirements for temple attendance do not change from place to place. Where a temple is available, priesthood authority gives no greater or lesser blessings in one place than another. Temple worship is a perfect example of our unity as Church members. All of us answer the same questions of worthiness to enter the temple. In the temple, all the men dress alike. All the women dress alike. We leave the cares of the world behind us as we enter the temple. Everyone receives the same blessings. All make the same covenants. All are equal before the Lord. Yet within our spiritual unity there is wide room for everyone's individuality and expression. In that setting, all are heirs to the kingdom of God. President Howard W. Hunter said it well: "The key to a unified church is a unified soul, one that is at peace with itself and not given to inner conflicts and tensions."[3]

The spiritual richness of our meetings seems to have little to do with the buildings or the country in which we meet. Many years ago, we went to Manaus, Brazil, a city far upstream on the Amazon River, surrounded by jungle, to meet with the missionaries and the handful of Saints who were then in that area. We met in a very humble home with no glass panes in the windows. The weather was excessively hot. The children sat on the floor. The mission president, President Helio Da Rocha Camargo, conducted the meeting and called on a faithful brother to give the opening prayer. The humble man responded, "I will be happy to pray, but may I also bear my testimony?" A sister was asked to lead the singing. She responded, "I would love to lead the singing, but please let me also bear my testimony."

And so it was all through the meeting with those who participated in any way. All felt impelled to bear their profound witness of the Savior and his mission and of the restoration of the gospel of Jesus Christ. All who were there reached deep down in their souls to their spiritual taproots, remembering the Savior's words that "where two or three are gathered together in my name, there am I in the midst of them" (Matthew 18:20). This they did more as heirs to the kingdom of God than as Brazilian members of the Church.

The multiplicity of languages and cultures is both an opportunity and a challenge for members of the Church. Having everyone hear the gospel in their own tongue requires great effort and resources. The Spirit, however, is a higher form of communication than language. We have been in many meetings where the words were completely unintelligible, but the Spirit bore powerful witness of Jesus Christ, the Savior and Redeemer of the world. Even with language differences, hopefully no minority group would ever feel so unwelcome in the "body of Christ" (see 1 Corinthians 10:16–17) that they would wish to worship exclusively in their own ethnic culture. We hope that those in any dominant culture would reach out to them in the brotherhood and sisterhood of the gospel so that we can establish fully a community of Saints where everyone will feel needed and wanted.

Spiritual peace is not to be found in race or culture or nationality but rather through our commitment to God and to the covenants and ordinances of the gospel. All of us, regardless of our nationality, need to reach down into the innermost recesses of our souls to find the divinity that is deep within us and to earnestly petition the Lord for an endowment of special wisdom and inspiration. Only when we so profoundly reach the depths of our beings can we discover our true identity, our self-worth, and our purpose in life. Only as we seek to be purged of selfishness and of concern for recognition and wealth can we find some sweet relief from the anxieties, hurts, pains, miseries, and concerns of this world. In this manner, as President J. Reuben Clark Jr. said, we can bring "to flower and fruitage the latent richness of the spirit."[4] God can not only help us find a sublime and everlasting joy and contentment, but he will change us so that we can become heirs of the kingdom of God.

This is really the recovery of the sacred within us. We have the authority in our beings to respond to challenges of life any way we choose. Thus we gain mastery in any circumstance. As the Savior said to the diseased woman, "Thy faith hath made thee whole" (Matthew 9:22).

Mine is the certain knowledge that Jesus is our divine Savior, Redeemer, and the Son of God the Father. I know of his reality by a sure perception so sacred I cannot give utterance to it. I know and testify with an absolute awareness that Joseph Smith restored the

Children of Christ, Heirs to the Kingdom of God

keys of the fulness of times and that every President of the Church has held these keys, as does President Gordon B. Hinckley today.

NOTES

1. "Helping Hearts and Hands Span the Globe," *Church News,* 11 February 1995, pp. 8–10.
2. In Conference Report, October 1963, p. 7.
3. *That We Might Have Joy* (Salt Lake City: Deseret Book Co., 1994), p. 50.
4. As cited in *Providing in the Lord's Way: A Leader's Guide to Welfare* (Salt Lake City: The Church of Jesus Christ of Latter-day Saints, 1990), p. i.

PART TWO

"LET YOUR LIGHT SO SHINE"
The Power of Example

CHAPTER SIX

Five Loaves and Two Fishes

Sᴏᴍᴇ ᴛɪᴍᴇ ᴀɢᴏ, as Elder Spencer J. Condie and I were in the Salt Lake airport, we unexpectedly met a devoted and faithful couple who have been friends for many years. This couple has spent a lifetime of service meekly, faithfully, and effectively trying to build up the Church in many places in the world. Elder Condie noted, "Isn't it remarkable what people with five loaves and two fishes do to build up the kingdom of God?" This kind of quiet, devoted service is surely a fulfillment of the word of God "that the fulness of my gospel might be proclaimed by the weak and the simple unto the ends of the world, and before kings and rulers" (D&C 1:23). I would like to write of those of us who have talents equal to only five loaves and two fishes to offer the Savior to help feed the multitudes.

> When Jesus then lifted up his eyes, and saw a great company come unto him, he saith unto Philip, Whence shall we buy bread, that these may eat?
> And this he said to prove him: for he himself knew what he would do. (John 6:5–6)

Philip answered quickly that there was not enough money to buy bread for the multitude. Then Andrew, Peter's brother, said, "There is a lad here, which hath five barley loaves, and two small fishes" (verse 9).

And when he had taken the five loaves and the two

fishes, he looked up to heaven, and blessed, and brake the loaves, and gave them to his disciples to set before them; and the two fishes divided he among them all.

And they did all eat, and were filled.

And they took up twelve baskets full of the fragments, and of the fishes.

And they that did eat of the loaves were about five thousand men. (Mark 6:41–44)

Subsequently their hearts were hardened in that they forgot the divine mission of Jesus, "for they considered not the miracle of the loaves" (verse 52).

In our time, we seem to have forgotten the miracle of the five loaves and the two fishes in favor of the miracles wrought by the mind and hand of men. I refer to the marvels of modern transportation and the increasing sophistication of all scientific knowledge, including the new electronic highway. We have forgotten that this amazing knowledge comes to mankind only as God chooses to reveal it, and it should be used for purposes nobler and wiser than mere entertainment. This knowledge permits the words of the prophets of God to be bounced off satellites hovering over the earth so it is possible for much of mankind to hear their messages.

With this great knowledge has come also some skepticism about the simple and profound eternal truths taught in the miracle of the loaves and of the fishes—namely, that God rules in the heavens and the earth through his infinite intelligence and goodness.

We are also to understand and remember that we too, like the lad in the New Testament account, are the spirit children of our Heavenly Father and that Jesus is the Christ, our Savior, and the Redeemer of the world. We believe that in the centuries following the establishment of his kingdom upon the earth, the doctrines and the ordinances were changed, resulting in a falling away and the loss of the keys of priesthood authority from the earth.

A miracle even greater than that of the loaves and the fishes was the vision of the Prophet Joseph Smith, who saw the Father and the Son in the Sacred Grove near Palmyra, New York. Subsequently the keys, the priesthood, and the saving ordinances were restored in their fulness, and Christ's church was reestablished in our time. Thus God has again fed us and filled our baskets to overflowing.

It has been said that this church does not necessarily attract great people but more often makes ordinary people great. Many people with little-known names and with gifts equal only to five loaves and two small fishes magnify their callings and serve without attention or recognition, feeding literally thousands. In large measure, they make possible the fulfillment of Nebuchadnezzar's dream that the latter-day gospel of Christ would be like a stone cut out of the mountain without hands, rolling forth until it fills the whole earth (see Daniel 2:34–35; D&C 65:2).

These are the hundreds of thousands of leaders and teachers in all of the auxiliaries and priesthood quorums, the home teachers, the Relief Society visiting teachers. These are the many humble bishops in the Church, some without formal training but greatly magnified, always learning, with a humble desire to serve the Lord and the people of their wards.

Any man or woman who enjoys the Master's touch is like potter's clay in his hands. More important than acquiring fame or fortune is being what God wants us to be. Before we came to this earth, we may have been fashioned to do some small good in this life that no one else can do. The Lord said to Jeremiah, "Before I formed thee in the belly I knew thee; and before thou camest forth out of the womb I sanctified thee, and I ordained thee a prophet unto the nations" (Jeremiah 1:5). If God has a work for those with many talents, I believe he also has an important work for those of us who have few.

What is the central characteristic of those having only five loaves and two fishes? What makes it possible, under the Master's touch, for them to serve, lift, and bless so that they touch for good the lives of hundreds, even thousands? After a lifetime of dealing in the affairs of men and women, I believe it is the ability to overcome personal ego and pride; both are enemies to the full enjoyment of the Spirit of God and to walking humbly before him. The ego interferes when husbands and wives fail to ask each other for forgiveness. It prevents the enjoyment of the full sweetness of a higher love. The ego often prevents parents and children from fully understanding one another. The ego enlarges our feelings of self-importance and worth. It blinds us to reality. Pride keeps us from confessing our sins and shortcomings to the Lord and working out our repentance.

What of those who have talents equal only to two loaves and one fish? They do much of the hard, menial, unchallenging, poorly compensated work of the world. Life may not have been quite fair to them. They struggle to have enough to hold body and soul together. But they are not forgotten. If their talents are used to build the kingdom of God and serve others, they will fully enjoy the promises of the Savior. The great promise of the Savior is that they "shall receive [their] reward, even peace in this world, and eternal life in the world to come" (D&C 59:23). The one who had only two talents was able to say, "Lord, thou deliveredst unto me two talents: behold, I have gained two other talents beside them." Thus said the Lord, "Well done, good and faithful servant; thou hast been faithful over a few things, I will make thee ruler over many things: enter . . . into the joy of thy lord" (Matthew 25:22–23).

It is a blessing for some to be given minds and talents equal to fifteen loaves and ten fishes. They have so very much that they can contribute, but some become less than they might. They do not reach their potential of service, perhaps because they take so much pride in what they think they know and what they have. They seem unwilling or unable to yield "to the enticings of the Holy Spirit . . . and [become] as a child, submissive, meek, humble, patient, full of love, willing to submit to all things which the Lord seeth fit to inflict upon [them], even as a child doth submit to his father" (Mosiah 3:19).

During much of my life, a few journalists and dissidents have

Five Loaves and Two Fishes

predicted the imminent downfall of this church. They have often pointed to the alleged disaffection of the youth of the Church. The lives and the dedication of our almost fifty thousand young missionaries are testament enough of the faithfulness of many of our youth. In addition, during my lifetime the Church has grown from 525,000 members to more than 9 million. I believe and testify that this is because of the restoration of the fulness of the keys and authority of the gospel of Christ to Joseph Smith.

Recently an out-of-state journalist used the phrase that there were appearing "cracks in the walls of the temple," figuratively speaking, of course. By this I suppose he meant that the moorings of the Church were being shaken by a very few who do not fully sustain the leaders of the Church or keep their covenants. To dispel this perception of cracks in our members' faith, we need only to observe the joyful people who worship in any of our forty-seven temples worldwide. Many are couples clutching their little bags and holding hands, and many are the unmarried, seeking the peaceful blessings of the house of the Lord. Their countenances reflect much joy and satisfaction in their lives.

A major reason this church has grown from its humble beginnings to its current strength is the faithfulness and devotion of millions of humble people who have only five loaves and two small fishes to offer in the service of the Master. They have largely surrendered their own interests and in so doing have found "the peace of God, which passeth all understanding" (Philippians 4:7). I wish only to be one of those who experience this supernal inner peace.

Jeff and Joyce Underwood of Pocatello, Idaho, are the parents of Jeralee and five other children. Jeff works on a building maintenance team that cares for some of our chapels in Pocatello. Joyce is a mother and homemaker. One day in July 1993, their daughter Jeralee, age eleven, was going door-to-door collecting money for her newspaper route. Jeralee never returned home—not that day, nor the next day, nor the next, nor ever.

Two thousand people from the area went out day after day to

search for her. Other churches sent support and food for the searchers. It was learned that Jeralee had been abducted and brutally murdered by an evil man. When her body was found, the whole city was horrified and shocked. All segments of the community reached out to Joyce and Jeff in love and sympathy. Some became angry and wanted to take vengeance.

After Jeralee's body was found, Jeff and Joyce appeared with great composure before the television cameras and other media to publicly express their profound thanks to all who had helped in the search and who had extended sympathy and love. Joyce said, "I know our Heavenly Father has heard and answered our prayers, and he has brought our daughter back to us." Jeff said, "We no longer have doubt about where she is." Joyce continued, "I have learned a lot about love this week, and I also know there is a lot of hate. I have looked at the love and want to feel that love, and not the hate. We can forgive."

Elder Joe J. Christensen and I, representing the General Authorities, were among the thousands privileged to attend Jeralee's funeral service. The Holy Spirit blessed that gathering in a remarkable way and spoke peace to the souls of all who attended. Later, President Kert W. Howard, Jeralee's stake president, wrote, "The Underwoods have received letters from people both in and out of the Church stating that they prayed for Jeralee, and they hadn't prayed in years, and because of this, they had a renewed desire to return to the Church." President Howard continued, "We will never know the extent of activation and rededication this single event has caused. Who knows the far-reaching effects Jeralee's life will have for generations untold?" Many have come into the Church because they wanted to know what kind of religion could give the Underwoods their spiritual strength.

I write of the good coming from this tragic event with Jeralee's parents' full approval and encouragement. Their sweet daughter was like the lad who had only five barley loaves and two small fishes

Five Loaves and Two Fishes

to give to the cause of the Savior, but by the power of God, countless thousands have been spiritually fed.

I testify that the gospel we teach is the "power of God unto salvation" for all who listen and obey (Romans 1:16), regardless of their talents and abilities.

CHAPTER SEVEN

A Legacy of Faith

THROUGHOUT THE WORLD, pioneers in the gospel have left us a priceless heritage. I acknowledge the faithful pioneers in all of the countries of the world who have helped establish the Church in their lands. First-generation members of the Church are indeed pioneers. They are and have been men and women of deep faith and devotion. Some of the great pioneers of the past, who left us a priceless legacy that belongs to the descendants of all pioneers, are those who came into the Salt Lake Valley and settled in Utah and other parts of western America.

Several years ago, in celebration of Pioneer Day on July 24, we joined the Saints of the Riverton Wyoming Stake. Under the direction of President Robert Lorimer and his counselors, the youth and youth leaders of that stake reenacted part of the handcart trek that took place in 1856. We started early in a four-wheel-drive van and went first to Independence Rock, where we began traveling along the Mormon Trail. We saw Devil's Gate a few miles up the road. Our souls were subdued when we arrived at the hallowed ground of Martin's Cove, the site where the Martin Handcart Company, freezing and starving, waited for the rescue wagons to come from Salt Lake City. Fifty-six members of the Martin Handcart Company perished there from hunger and cold.

It was an emotional experience to see the Sweetwater River crossing where most of the five hundred members of the company were carried across the icy river by three brave young men. Later, all three of the boys died from the effects of the terrible strain and great exposure experienced during that crossing. "When President Brigham Young heard of this heroic act, he wept like a child and later declared publicly: 'That act alone will ensure C. Allen Huntington, George W. Grant and David P. Kimball an everlasting salvation in the Celestial Kingdom of God, worlds without end.'"[1]

We went farther along the trail to the site where the members of the Willie Handcart Company were rescued. We felt that we were standing on holy ground. At that site twenty-one members of that party died from starvation and cold. We continued to travel up over Rocky Ridge, seventy-three hundred feet high. This is the highest spot on the Mormon Trail. The two-mile ascension to Rocky Ridge gains over seven hundred feet in altitude. It was very difficult for all of the pioneers to travel over Rocky Ridge. It was particularly agonizing for the members of the Willie Handcart Company, who struggled over that ridge in the fall of 1856 in a blizzard. Many had worn-out shoes, and the sharp rocks caused their feet to bleed, leaving a trail of blood in the snow.

As we walked over Rocky Ridge, two square nails and an old-style button were picked up. No doubt these objects were shaken loose going over the sharp rocks. My soul was sobered to be in that historic spot. Several of my ancestors crossed that ridge, though none were in the handcart companies. Not all of my forebears who started in the great exodus to the West made it even to the Rocky Ridge. Two of them died at Winter Quarters.

As I walked over Rocky Ridge, I wondered if I have sacrificed enough. In my generation I have not seen so much sacrifice by so many. I wonder what more I should have done, and should be doing, to further this work.

A few miles farther, at Radium Springs, we caught up with 185 young people and their leaders from the Riverton stake who had been pulling handcarts in reenactment of the handcart treks. We

A Legacy of Faith

bore testimony of the faith and heroism of those who struggled in agony over that trail so many years ago.

We went on to Rock Creek Hollow, where the Willie Handcart Company made camp. Thirteen members of the Willie company who perished from cold, exhaustion, and starvation are buried in a common grave at Rock Creek Hollow. Two additional members who died during the night are buried nearby. Two of those buried at Rock Creek Hollow were heroic children of tender years: Bodil Mortinsen, age nine, from Denmark, and James Kirkwood, age eleven, from Scotland.

Bodil apparently was assigned to care for some small children as they crossed Rocky Ridge. When they arrived at camp, she must have been sent to gather firewood. She was found frozen to death leaning against the wheel of her handcart, clutching sagebrush.

Let me tell you of James Kirkwood. James was from Glasgow, Scotland. On the trip west, James was accompanied by his widowed mother and three brothers, one of whom, Thomas, was nineteen and crippled and had to ride in the handcart. James's primary responsibility on the trek was to care for his little four-year-old brother, Joseph, while his mother and oldest brother, Robert, pulled the cart. As they climbed Rocky Ridge, it was snowing and there was a bitter cold wind blowing. It took the whole company twenty-seven hours to travel fifteen miles. When little Joseph became too weary to walk, James, the older brother, had no choice but to carry him. Left behind the main group, James and Joseph made their way slowly to camp. When the two finally arrived at the fireside, James, "having so faithfully carried out his task, collapsed and died from exposure and over-exertion."[2]

Also heroic were the rescuers who responded to President Brigham Young's call in the October 1856 general conference. President Young called for forty young men, sixty to sixty-five teams of mules or horses, and wagons loaded with twenty-four thousand pounds of flour to leave in the next day or two to *bring in those people now on the plains.*"³ The rescuers went swiftly to relieve the suffering travelers.

When the rescued sufferers got close to the Salt Lake Valley, Brigham Young convened a meeting. He directed the Saints in the valley to receive the sufferers into their homes, make them comfortable, and administer food and clothing to them. Said President Young: "Some you will find with their feet frozen to their ankles; some are frozen to their knees and some have their hands frosted. . . . We want you to receive them as your own children, and to have the same feeling for them."⁴

When the rescuers brought the Willie handcart pioneers into this valley, it is recorded by Captain Willie: "On our arrival there the Bishops of the different Wards took every person, who was not provided with a home, to comfortable quarters. Some had their hands and feet badly frozen; but everything which could be done to alleviate their sufferings, was done. . . . Hundreds of the Citizens flocked round the wagons on our way through the City, cordially welcoming their Brethren and Sisters to their mountain home."⁵

These excruciating experiences developed in these pioneers an unshakable faith in God. Said Elizabeth Horrocks Jackson Kingsford, "But I believe the Recording Angel has inscribed in the archives above, and that my sufferings for the Gospel's sake will be sanctified unto me for my good."⁶

In addition to the legacy of faith bequeathed by those who crossed the plains, they also left a great heritage of love—love of God and love of mankind. It is an inheritance of sobriety, independence, hard work, high moral values, and fellowship. It is a birthright of obedience to the commandments of God and loyalty to those whom God has called to lead this people. It is a legacy of forsaking evil. Immorality, alternative lifestyles, gambling, selfishness, dishonesty, unkindness, and addiction to alcohol and drugs are not part of the gospel of Jesus Christ.

From time to time, Latter-day Saints, as citizens of the various nations, have the opportunity to vote on issues that are not only

A Legacy of Faith

political but also moral issues. The Church is not retreating from its stand on these issues. But as contests and issues heat up, we counsel members of the Church to be tolerant and understanding. We all have our moral agency, but if we use it unwisely, we must pay the price. President J. Reuben Clark Jr. said, "We may use our agency as to whether we shall obey or disobey; and if we disobey we must abide the penalty."[7]

I cannot help wondering why these intrepid pioneers had to pay for their faith with such a terrible price in agony and suffering. Why were not the elements tempered to spare them from their profound agony? I believe their lives were consecrated to a higher purpose through their suffering. Their love for the Savior was burned deep into their souls and into the souls of their children and their children's children. The motivation for their lives came from a true conversion in the center of their souls. As President Gordon B. Hinckley has said, "When there throbs in the heart of an individual Latter-day Saint a great and vital testimony of the truth of this work, he will be found doing his duty in the Church."[8]

Above and beyond the epic historical events they participated in, the pioneers found a guide to personal living. They found reality and meaning in their lives. In the difficult days of their journey, the members of the Martin and Willie handcart companies encountered some apostates from the Church who were returning from the West, going back to the East. These apostates tried to persuade some in the companies to turn back. A few did turn back. But the great majority of the pioneers went forward to a heroic achievement in this life and to eternal life in the life hereafter.

Francis Webster, a member of the Martin Handcart Company, stated, *"Everyone of us came through with the absolute knowledge that God lives for we became acquainted with him in our extremities."*[9] I hope that this priceless legacy of faith left by the pioneers will inspire all of us to more fully participate in the Savior's work of bringing to pass the immortality and eternal life of his children.

You who are among the descendants of these noble pioneers

have a priceless heritage of faith and courage. If there are any of you who do not enjoy fellowship with us in the gospel of Jesus Christ, we invite you to seek to know what instilled such great faith in your ancestors and what motivated them to willingly pay such a terrible price for their membership in this church. To those who have been offended or lost interest or who have turned away for any reason, we invite all of you to join in full fellowship again with us. The faithful members, with all their faults and failings, are humbly striving to do God's holy work across the world. We need your help in the great struggle against the powers of darkness so prevalent in the world today. In becoming a part of this work, you can all satisfy the deepest yearnings of your souls. You can come to know the personal comfort that can be found in seeking the sacred and holy things of God. You can enjoy the blessings and covenants administered in the holy temples. You can have great meaning and purpose in your lives, even in the profane world in which we live. You can have strength of character so that you can act for yourselves and not be acted upon (see 2 Nephi 2:26).

A few years ago the First Presidency of the Church issued the invitation to all to come back:

> We are aware of some who are inactive, of others who have become critical and are prone to find fault, and of those who have been disfellowshipped or excommunicated because of serious transgressions.
>
> To all such we reach out in love. We are anxious to forgive in the spirit of Him who said: "I, the Lord, will forgive whom I will forgive, but of you it is required to forgive all men." (D&C 64:10)
>
> We encourage Church members to forgive those who may have wronged them. To those who have ceased activity and to those who have become critical, we say, "Come back. Come back and feast at the table of the Lord, and taste again the sweet and satisfying fruits of fellowship with the saints."
>
> We are confident that many have [wanted] to return, but

A Legacy of Faith

have felt awkward about doing so. We assure you that you will find open arms to receive you and willing hands to assist you.[10]

On behalf of my Brethren, I sincerely and humbly reiterate that request. And we open our arms to you.

NOTES

1. Solomon F. Kimball, "Belated Emigrants of 1856," *Improvement Era,* February 1914, p. 288.

2. Private letter, Don H. Smith to Robert Lorimer, 20 February 1990, quoting account of Don Chislett.

3. LeRoy R. Hafen and Ann W. Hafen, *Handcarts to Zion* (Glendale, California: Arthur H. Clark Co., 1960), p. 121; italics in original.

4. Hafen, *Handcarts to Zion,* p. 139.

5. James G. Willie, in *Journal History of The Church of Jesus Christ of Latter-day Saints,* 9 November 1856, p. 15.

6. *Leaves from the Life of Elizabeth Horrocks Jackson Kingsford* (Ogden, Utah: n.p., 1908), p. 7.

7. *Fundamentals of the Church Welfare Plan* (address at bishops' meeting, 6 October 1944), p. 3.

8. *Ensign,* May 1984, p. 99.

9. As quoted in David O. McKay, "Pioneer Women," *Relief Society Magazine,* January 1948, p. 8; italics in original.

10. "An Invitation to Come Back," *Church News,* 22 December 1985, p. 3.

CHAPTER EIGHT

A New Civil Religion

N EARLY 150 YEARS AGO, the first company of Mormon pioneers was in the area known as Hennefer, Utah. On that day they climbed the ridge known as Hogs Back Summit, which was dangerous and difficult for the wagons. Wilford Woodruff called it "the worst road we have had on the journey." The wheels of George A. Smith's wagon collapsed inward, zigzagging down from the summit. In the evening Orson Pratt and his advance party were on Big Mountain looking through an opening in the canyons. It was the pioneers' first glimpse of the valley of the Great Salt Lake.[1]

In the state of Utah, Latter-day Saints memorialize each year those valiant pioneers who settled Utah and the surrounding areas. They were a people persecuted and driven out of what was then the United States because of their religious beliefs. They came west seeking to worship Almighty God according to the dictates of their own conscience.

Almost three centuries before, in a like manner, God-fearing believers, most notable of which were the Pilgrims, left Europe with its state religions and came to this land to seek freedom of worship. As a consequence of this, the deepest taproots of the United States and the state of Utah in the past have lain in the very essence of our humanity; our faith in God. Some U.S. coins still contain the phrase "In God We Trust." Our pledge of allegiance states that we are "one nation under God, indivisible, with liberty and justice for all."

"Let Your Light So Shine"

The recent controversy in the United States of America regarding the constitutionality of certain public prayers casts a serious cloud over the reality and meaning of the sacred in our society.

There seems to be developing a new civil religion. The civil religion I refer to is a secular religion. It has no moral absolutes. It is nondenominational. It is nontheistic. It is politically focused. It is antagonistic to religion. It rejects the historic religious traditions of the nation. It feels strange. If this trend continues, nonbelief will be more honored than belief. While all beliefs must be protected, are atheism, agnosticism, cynicism, and moral relativism to be more safeguarded and valued than Christianity, Judaism, and the tenets of Islam, which hold that there is a Supreme Being and that mortals are accountable to him? If so, this would, in my opinion, place the United States of America in great moral jeopardy.

For those who believe in God, this new civil religion fosters some of the same concerns as the state religions that prompted our forefathers to escape to the New World. Nonbelief is becoming more sponsored in the body politic than belief. I believe there is great danger in this to the nation. History teaches the lesson well that there must be a unity in some moral absolutes in all societies for them to endure and progress. Indeed, without a national morality they disintegrate. Proverbs reminds us that "righteousness exalteth a nation: but sin is a reproach to any people" (Proverbs 14:34). The long history and tradition of this nation, which had its roots in petitions for divine guidance, is being challenged.

On this issue Justice Oliver Wendell Holmes commented that "a page of history is worth a volume of logic."[2] Appeals for divine guidance, forgiveness, and approbation have been part of the fabric of this nation from the beginning. The first prayer in Congress was offered in September 1774. In his farewell address, George Washington acknowledged that "of all the dispositions and habits which lead to political prosperity, religion and morality are indispensable supports. . . . Reason and experience both forbid us to expect that national morality can prevail in exclusion of religious principle."

Similarly, Abraham Lincoln declared, "God rules this world—it is the duty of nations as well as men to own their dependence upon the overruling power of God, to confess their sins and transgressions in humble sorrow . . . and to recognize the sublime truth that those nations only are blessed whose God is their Lord."

Thomas Jefferson, in his first inaugural address, prayed, "May that infinite power which rules the destinies of the universe lead our councils to do what is best and give them a favorable issue for your peace and prosperity."

James Madison, in his first inaugural address, stated that his confidence was "in the guardianship and guidance of that Mighty Being whose power regulates the destiny of nations, whose blessings have been so conspicuously dispensed to this rising Republic, and to whom we are bound to address our devout gratitude for the past, as well as our fervent supplications and best hopes for the future."

Every session of the United States Supreme Court to this day opens with the plea, "God save the United States and this honorable court."

In the Book of Mormon, Moroni gives the inhabitants of this nation a stern warning: "For behold, this is a land which is choice above all other lands; wherefore he that doth possess it shall serve God or shall be swept off; for it is the everlasting decree of God" (Ether 2:10).

The new civil religion is different from that envisioned by Benjamin Franklin, who seems to have first discussed the concept of "civil religion."[3] Franklin's civil religion, as I understand it, was envisioned to replace the state religions of Europe, with their forced taxation and oppression. Franklin no doubt envisioned that this vacuum would be filled with a patriotism reflected by national symbolism, pride, ethics, values, and purpose. His eloquent statement concerning divine intervention in the Constitutional Convention clearly indicated he was not opposed to religiosity.

The new civil religion isn't really a religion as you and I would use that term to describe a faith or a church or synagogue that worships Almighty God and espouses a code of moral conduct for its adherents. This new civil religion teaches a sectarian philosophy that is hostile to traditional religion. It has its own orthodoxy. It could even end up in an ironic violation of the Federal Constitution, which states that there shall be no religious basis for office.[4] Will irreligion become a test for office? May I share with you several examples that illustrate this?

Every American has been taught that the "freedom of religion" is the "first freedom" guaranteed by the Bill of Rights. The First Amendment to the Constitution recognizes the "free exercise of religion" as the preeminent position among constitutional rights as intended by the Founding Fathers.

Most Americans are unaware, however, that several years ago this most fundamental right was substantially eroded. For decades, whenever government tried to pass laws that interfered with any right guaranteed under the Constitution, the law was given careful scrutiny by the courts. Government was required to show that first, it had a "compelling governmental interest" that justified the interference with a Constitutional right, and second, that this "compelling governmental interest" could not be achieved through some other, less intrusive means. This strict scrutiny rule of law was even applied to rights that have been created by the courts even though they are not specifically found in the Constitution—such as the right to privacy, which is the basis for the legalization of abortion.

In the case of *Oregon Employment Division v. Smith*,[5] however, this strict scrutiny and the burden on government to demonstrate a "compelling interest" was abandoned in cases involving the free exercise of religion. According to the court, religious exclusions to public policy is "a luxury we can no longer afford."

As a result, any government (federal, state, or local) was able to pass any law that infringed upon individual religious liberty as long as the law applied generally to everyone. In California, for example, a Catholic couple was sued in federal court because they refused, on religious and moral grounds, to rent an apartment in their own home to an unmarried couple living together.

A Quaker employer whose religious beliefs demand that he welcome the sojourner and the poor was denied relief from the Immigration Reform and Control Act.[6]

An autopsy was performed on a Hmong boy against the religious beliefs of his parents, who believed that mutilating his body would prevent his spirit from becoming free.[7]

The Civil Rights Act of 1964 has been construed to require the Boy Scouts of America to admit into membership persons who are unwilling to profess a belief in God.[8]

As a result of the case *Oregon Employment Division v. Smith,* Congress passed the Religious Freedom Restoration Act by an overwhelming margin, and the act was signed into law on November 16, 1993. This act restored the requirement of the government to prove that there is a compelling state interest before interfering with the free exercise of religion. Unfortunately, the constitutionality of the Religious Freedom Restoration Act is now being brought into question.

The civil secular religion also teaches that the establishment clause of the First Amendment—companion to the "free exercise" clause—should be applied to prevent religious organizations from working cooperatively with the government to bring about worthwhile public policy. There are many laudatory public purposes, such as education, literacy, public health, welfare, and assistance to the poor where charitable institutions, including churches, can and should work with government assistance programs for the public good.

There are numerous examples, however, of instances in which governments have tried, through tax incentives, grants of educational materials or other commodities, to provide accommodation to religious institutions that provide public service—only to be challenged in court for fostering religion in violation of the establishment clause.

Another governmental accommodation that could be honored is the religious feelings of the people for matters such as religious holidays and traditions. These involve little public financial assistance but are frequently challenged as a violation of establishment.

I have chosen to emphasize this subject because the twin religious clauses of the Bill of Rights—"Congress shall make no law respecting an establishment of religion, or prohibiting the free exercise thereof"[9]—are golden threads that in the past have permitted those who believe in God to publicly affirm that there is a higher power that "rules in the affairs of men." These religious clauses have fostered the creative impulses and the vitality of religion in an open, heterogeneous society. These clauses have freed this country from the terrible religious violence that has existed in Europe over the centuries and from which our forefathers in this country sought to escape. One author described these religious clauses in the Constitution as "the Articles of Peace."[10]

The establishment and free exercise clauses should be read together to harmonize the importance of religious liberty with freedom from government regulation. Rather, today, in my opinion, the establishment clause is being used in our nation to restrict religious institutions from playing a role in civic issues, and the free exercise clause denies to individuals their religious liberty. It does not accord the equivalent to what the Constitution accords to secularism—the new civil religion.

One basic difference between Franklin's concept of a civil religion and the new secular religion is that the new secular religion rejects in large measure the basic concept of Anglo-Saxon-American jurisprudence. Our traditional jurisprudence has held that God is the source of all of our basic rights and that the principal function of government is only to secure those rights for its citizenry. May I quote from the Declaration of Independence: "We hold these truths to be self-evident, that all men are created equal; that they are endowed by their Creator with certain inalienable rights; . . . that to secure these rights, governments are instituted among men."

In contrast, the new civil religion I speak of finds its source of rights by invoking the power of the state. It seems to have little purpose and few common values for morality except self-interest. Recently that power was invoked by the Supreme Court in a case known in legal circles as *Lee v. Weisman*. This is the case that resulted in the Supreme Court's banning ceremonial prayer at public school exercises. Commenting on the case, Edwin Yoder, distinguished columnist for the *Washington Post,* observed that "this decision is more than a natural extension of the original school prayer decision of 1962. It more closely resembles a promotion of secularity in the public forum—a result which some framers of the First Amendment Establishment Clause probably did not so much as dream of."

Yoder further states: "Religion has a legitimate public, ceremonial and community function which may be stunted by such decisions. It is far from clear why children, even of tender years, need to be protected from religion even on special ceremonial occasions."[11]

There are natural safeguards in a God-fearing people that promote respect for law and order, decency, and public civility. One such restraining influence is the belief that the citizenry will be accountable to their Creator for their conduct under a high moral law. This respect for and adherence to moral law transcends the constraints of the civil and criminal codes. In a people who are not God-fearing, however, these characteristics are notably absent.

Will public civility be lost under the guise of claiming under Constitutional safeguards the rights to freedom of speech? Will tolerance of other faiths and beliefs continue to be diminished by claiming rights under the establishment and free exercise clauses of the Constitution?

Several years ago during the Los Angeles riots, we viewed our countrymen in Los Angeles lawlessly looting business establishments and happily carrying out stolen goods. When viewing the daily television fare and when confronted with the overwhelming social ills of this country, we can hardly say that our citizenry have been overexposed to moral teachings. One of the responsibilities of government under their police powers is to protect the health, safety, and morals of the citizenry. Our governments have not succeeded well in this duty of protecting morals, especially in regard to the coming generation.

Several kinds of moral evils have crawled inside the Constitutional fortress. Pornography, for example, finds its most effective shield in the First Amendment freedom of expression rights. The Constitutional freedom of conscience has been given a reverse twist with public prayer decisions.

The new civil religion is, in my opinion, coming dangerously close to becoming a *de facto* state religion of secularism. Litigation—and the fear of litigation—have made school boards and local governments reluctant to publicly defend moral principles. As a consequence, fewer public institutions are willing to take the stand in defense of moral values.

Historically in this nation the public religion was sacred rather than sectarian or secular. Public statements from the judicial as well as the legislative and executive branches affirmed a higher destiny for this nation under the providence of the Almighty. This is evidenced by Justice Brewer's pronouncement in 1892, "This is a Christian nation."[12] The sacred aspect of public religion of this country continued until 1946, when the secular was ushered in by a case called *Everson v. the Board of Education.*[13]

With the public religion now turning increasingly toward the secular, I wonder how this nation will preserve its enduring values. In my view, there is a substantial governmental interest within the

A New Civil Religion

limits of the religious clauses of the Constitution in public prayer and expressions of all faiths that acknowledge the existence of deity. Such prayer and expressions accommodate the abiding values shared by a great majority of our citizenry. They give meaning to a transcendent spiritual reality and idealism which, in the past at least, was quite firmly held by the people of our society. The very essence of our concern for human welfare and alleviation of human suffering lies in our spiritual feelings and expressions.

So now we find ourselves in a situation where, unlike the Pilgrims, the Mormon pioneers, and others, we have nowhere to go in order to escape a new civil *de facto* secular state religion that continually limits public religious expression and fosters secular values and expressions. How do we preserve the essence of our humanity?

Surely we must begin in our homes. We must teach our children and grandchildren. The moral teachings of all our churches must have an honored place in our society. The general decline in the moral fabric of the citizenry places a greater responsibility on homes and churches to teach values—morality, decency, respect for others, patriotism, and honoring and sustaining the law.

We can also exercise our right, with all other citizens, to vote for men and women who reflect our own values. We can also express our views as all other citizens have a right to do in the legislative process of both the state and the nation. With all others we can claim our rights of free expression. We can petition for the redress of grievances.

We can help educate the coming generation about their rights and duties. We can educate ourselves about the important moral issues of our time. There is no desert to flee to in order to have full freedom. There is no place across the waters for pilgrims. Therefore we must hold to our beliefs and do what we can.

NOTES

1. Hal Knight and Stanley B. Kimball, *111 Days to Zion* (Salt Lake City: *Deseret Press*, 1978), pp. 242–43.
2. *New York Trust Company v. Eisner,* 256 US 345, 349 (1921).

"Let Your Light So Shine"

3. Martin E. Marty, *Pilgrims in Their Own Land* (Boston: Little, Brown and Co., 1984), pp. 155–66.

4. Article VI, The Constitution of the United States of America.

5. *Oregon Employment Division v. Smith*, 110 Supreme Ct, 1595 (1990).

6. *American Friends Service Committee v. Thornburgh*, 951 F2d 957.

7. *Yang v. Sturner*, 750 FSupp 558.

8. *Welsh v. Boy Scouts of America*, 742 FSupp 1413.

9. First Amendment, The Constitution of the United States of America.

10. Father J. Murray, *We Hold These Truths*, p. 45.

11. *The Salt Lake Tribune*, 1 July 1992, p. A10.

12. *Church of the Holy Trinity v. US*, 143 US 457, 471 (1892).

13. *Everson v. the Board of Education*, 330 US 1.

CHAPTER NINE

Finding Light in a Dark World

SOMEONE SAID IN these few words: "I have heard much about the devil. I have read a great deal about the devil. I have even done business with the devil, but it didn't pay." We live in a day when many things are measured against the standard of social or political correctness. I challenge that false doctrine of human behavior. The influence of Satan is becoming more acceptable. Elizabeth Barrett Browning said, "The devil's most devilish when respectable."[1] However, as Shakespeare said, "He's mad that trusts in the tameness of a wolf."[2]

It is not good practice to become intrigued by Satan and his mysteries. No good can come from getting close to evil. As when playing with fire, it is too easy to get burned: "The knowledge of sin tempteth to its commission."[3] The only safe course is to keep well distanced from him and from any of his wicked activities or nefarious practices. The mischief of devil worship, sorcery, casting spells, witchcraft, voodooism, black magic, and all other forms of demonism should be avoided.

However, Brigham Young said that it is important to "study . . . evil, and its consequences."[4] Since Satan is the author of all evil in the world, it would therefore be essential to realize that he is the influence behind the opposition to the work of God. Alma stated the issue succinctly: "For I say unto you that whatsoever is good cometh from God, and whatsoever is evil cometh from the devil" (Alma 5:40).

I owe my text to Elder Marion G. Romney who, at a Brigham Young University devotional in 1955, stated: "Now there are those among us who are trying to serve the Lord without offending the devil." This is a contradiction of terms. President Romney goes on: "Must the choice lie irrevocably between peace on the one hand, obtained by compliance with the gospel of Jesus Christ as restored through the Prophet Joseph Smith, and contention and war on the other hand?"[5]

Yogi Berra is reported to have said, "If you come to a fork in the road, take it." But it doesn't work that way. The Savior said, "No man can serve two masters: for either he will hate the one, and love the other; or else he will hold to the one, and despise the other. Ye cannot serve God and mammon" (Matthew 6:24). Today many of us are trying to serve two masters—the Lord and our own selfish interests—without offending the devil. The influence of God, our Eternal Father, urges us, pleads with us, and inspires us to follow him. In contrast, the power of Satan urges us to disbelieve and disregard God's commandments.

President Romney continues: "The consequences of [mortal man's] choices are of the all-or-nothing sort. There is no way for him to escape the influence of these opposing powers. Inevitably he is led by one or the other. His God-given free agency gives him the power and option to choose. But choose he must. Nor can he serve both of them at the same time, for, as Jesus said, 'No man can serve two masters: . . . Ye cannot serve God and mammon.'"[6]

In the October 1987 general conference, I made this statement: I think we will witness increasing evidence of Satan's power as the kingdom of God grows stronger. I believe Satan's ever-expanding efforts are some proof of the truthfulness of this work. In the future, the opposition will be both more subtle and more open. It will be masked in greater sophistication and cunning, but it will also be more blatant. We will need greater spirituality to perceive all of the forms of evil and greater strength to resist it.

Abortion is one evil practice that has become socially accepted in our country and, indeed, in the world. Many of today's politicians claim not to favor abortion but oppose government intervention in a woman's right to choose an abortion.

During a national prayer breakfast in Washington on February 3, 1994, Mother Teresa gave the most honest and powerful proclamation of truth on this subject I have ever heard. She is the eighty-three-year-old Yugoslavian nun who has cared for the poorest of the poor in India for years. She is now aged and physically frail, but courageous, with immense spiritual strength. Mother Teresa delivered a message that cut to the very heart and soul of the social ills afflicting America, which traditionally has given generously to the peoples of the earth but now has become selfish. She stated that the greatest proof of that selfishness is abortion. Cal Thomas of the Los Angeles Times Syndicate reported the speech. He said that Mother Teresa had tied abortion to growing violence and murder in the streets by saying, "If we accept that a mother can kill even her own child, how can we tell other people not to kill each other? . . . Any country that accepts abortion is not teaching its people to love, but to use any violence to get what they want."[7]

Then she alluded to the concern that has been shown for orphan children in India and elsewhere in the world, for which she expressed gratitude. But she continued, "These concerns are very good. But often these same people are not concerned with the millions who are being killed by the deliberate decision of their own mothers. And this is what is the greatest destroyer of peace today—abortion, which brings people to such blindness."[8] Cal Thomas, commenting on this powerful message, said: "Why should people or nations regard human life as noble or dignified if abortion flourishes? Why agonize about indiscriminate death in Bosnia when babies are being killed far more efficiently and out of the sight of television cameras?"[9]

In conclusion Mother Teresa pled for pregnant women who don't want their children to give them to her. She said, "I am willing to accept any child who would be aborted and to give that child to a married couple who will love the child and be loved by the child."[10] What consummate spiritual courage this remarkable old woman demonstrated. How the devil must have been offended! Her remarkable declaration, however, was not generally picked up by the press or the editorial writers. Perhaps they felt more comfortable being politically or socially correct. After all, they can justify their stance by making excuses like "Everyone does it" or "It is legal." Fortunately the scriptures and the message of the prophets cannot be so revised.

I speak next of the present-day challenge to the words of the Lord recorded in Genesis: "Be fruitful, and multiply, and replenish the earth" (Genesis 1:28). All my life I have heard the argument that the earth is overpopulated. Much controversy surrounded a recently concluded United Nations International Conference on Population and Development held in Cairo, Egypt. No doubt the conference accomplished much that was worthwhile. But at the very center of the debate was the socially acceptable phrase "sustainable growth." This concept is becoming increasingly popular. How cleverly Satan masks his evil designs with that phrase.

Few voices in the developed nations cry out in the wilderness against this coined phrase "sustainable growth." In a recent issue of *Forbes Magazine,* a thoughtful editorial asserts that people are an asset, not a liability. It forthrightly declares as preposterous the broadly accepted premise that curbing population growth is essential for economic development. The editorial then states convincingly that "free people don't exhaust resources, they create them."[11]

An article in *U.S. News and World Report* states that the earth is capable of producing food for a population of at least eighty billion, eight times the ten billion expected to inhabit the earth by the year 2050. One study estimates that with improved scientific methods, the earth could feed as many as one thousand billion people.[12]

Those who argue for sustainable growth lack vision and faith. The Lord said, "For the earth is full, and there is enough and to spare" (D&C 104:17). That settles the issue for me. It should settle the issue for all of us. The Lord has spoken.

The Church's stand on homosexual relations provides another arena where we offend the devil. I expect that the statement of the First Presidency and the Twelve against homosexual marriages will continue to be assaulted. Satan is interested only in our misery, which he promotes by trying to persuade men and women to act contrary to God's plan. One way he does this is by encouraging the inappropriate use of sacred creative powers. A bona fide marriage is one between a man and a woman, one solemnized by the proper legal or ecclesiastical authority. Only sexual relations between husband and wife within the bonds of marriage are acceptable before the Lord.

There is some widely accepted theory extant that homosexuality is inherited. How can this be? No scientific evidence demonstrates absolutely that this is so. If it were, it would frustrate the whole plan of mortal happiness. Our designation as men or women began before this world was. In contrast to the socially accepted doctrine that homosexuality is inborn, a number of respectable authorities contend that homosexuality is not acquired by birth. The false belief of inborn sexual orientation denies to repentant souls the opportunity to change and will ultimately lead to discouragement, disappointment, and despair.

Any alternatives to the legal and loving marriage between a man and a woman will only threaten to unravel the fabric of human society. I am sure this is pleasing to the devil. The fabric I refer to is the family. These so-called alternative lifestyles must not be accepted as right; they frustrate God's commandment for a life-giving union of male and female within a legal marriage, as stated in Genesis. If practiced by all adults, these lifestyles would mean the end of the human family.

I suggest that the devil takes some delight every time a home is

"Let Your Light So Shine"

broken up, even where there is no parent to blame. This is especially so where there are children involved. The physical and spiritual neglect of children is one of the spawning grounds for so many of the social ills of the world.

I now turn to milder ways of not offending the devil. Nephi has given to us the pattern or formula by which Satan operates:

> And others will he pacify, and lull them away into carnal security, that they will say: All is well in Zion; yea, Zion prospereth, all is well—and thus the devil cheateth their souls, and leadeth them away carefully down to hell.
>
> And behold, others he flattereth away, and telleth them there is no hell; and he saith unto them: I am no devil, for there is none—and thus he whispereth in their ears, until he grasps them with his awful chains, from whence there is no deliverance. (2 Nephi 28:21–22)

C. S. Lewis gave us a keen insight into devilish tactics. In a fictional letter, the master devil, Screwtape, instructs the apprentice devil Wormwood, who is in training to become a more experienced devil:

> You will say that these are very small sins; and doubtless, like all young tempters, you are anxious to be able to report spectacular wickedness. . . . It does not matter how small the sins are, provided that their cumulative effect is to edge the man away from the Light and out into the Nothing. . . . Indeed, the safest road to Hell is the gradual one—the gentle slope, soft underfoot, without sudden turnings, without milestones, without signposts.[13]

So-called small sins include the challenge to the "sin laws" that seek to control forms of gambling, alcohol, and drug consumption. Some who wish to appear broad-minded say, under the guise of not imposing religious belief, "I don't drink or gamble, but I don't think we ought to have any laws to control others who wish to." This completely ignores the damage to the health of our fellowman and the social costs to society that are the results of these vices. "Broad-minded" individuals may foolishly argue that laws cannot control human behavior. My long legal career has led me to conclude that all criminal laws have a moral basis.

I now come to some even milder forms of trying to serve the Lord without offending the devil. Having a temple recommend and not using it seems mild enough. However, if we live close to a temple, perhaps having a temple recommend but not using it may not offend the devil. Satan is offended when we use that recommend, going to the temple to partake of the spiritual protection it affords. How often do we plan to go to the temple only to have all kinds of hindrances arise to stop us from going? The devil always has been offended by our temple worship. As President Brigham Young once said about the building of temples, there are Saints who say, "I do not like to do it, for we never began to build a temple without the bells of hell beginning to ring." His answer was, "I want to hear them ring again. All the tribes of hell will be on the move, if we uncover the walls of this temple."[14] President Howard W. Hunter said that we should "look to the temple of the Lord as the great symbol" of our Church membership.[15]

I wonder how much we offend Satan if the proclamation of our faith is limited only to the great humanitarian work this church does throughout the world or the building of our beautiful buildings, marvelous as these activities are. When we preach the gospel of social justice, no doubt the devil is not troubled. But I believe the devil is terribly offended when we boldly declare by personal testimony that Joseph Smith was a prophet of God and that he saw the Father and the Son; when we preach that the Book of Mormon is another witness for Christ; when we declare that there has been a restoration of the fulness of the gospel in its simplicity and power in order to fulfill the great plan of happiness.

We challenge the powers of darkness when we speak of the perfect life of the Savior and of his sublime work for all mankind through the Atonement. This supernal gift permits us, through repentance, to break away from Satan's grasping tentacles.

We please the devil when we argue that all roads lead to heaven and that, therefore, it does not matter which road we take, because we will all end up in God's presence. And he is no doubt pleased when we contend that we are all God's children; therefore, it makes no difference to which church a person belongs, because we are all working for the same place.

This man-made philosophy—for such it is—sounds good, but the scriptures do not support it. I assure each of you that the road to God's presence is not that easy. It is strait and narrow. Elder Delbert L. Stapley said, "I feel certain that the devil chuckles whenever this false opinion is expressed, for it pleases him that the minds of men have been so blinded to revealed truth by his cunning craftiness and deceit that they will believe any religion to be acceptable to God regardless of its tenets and ordinances or how or by whom those ordinances are administered."[16]

We have heard comedians and others justify or explain their misdeeds by saying, "The devil made me do it." I do not really think the devil can make us do anything. Certainly he can tempt and he can deceive, but he has no authority over us which we do not give him.

The power to resist Satan may be stronger than we realize. The Prophet Joseph Smith taught: "All beings who have bodies have power over those who have not. The devil has no power over us only as we permit him. The moment we revolt at anything which comes from God, the devil takes power."[17]

He also stated, "Wicked spirits have their bounds, limits, and laws by which they are governed."[18] So Satan and his angels are not all-powerful.

Satan has had great success with this gullible generation. As a consequence, literally hosts of people have been victimized by him and his angels. There is, however, an ample shield against the power of Lucifer and his hosts. This protection lies in the spirit of discernment through the gift of the Holy Ghost. This gift comes undeviatingly by personal revelation to those who strive to obey the

Finding Light in a Dark World

commandments of the Lord and to follow the counsel of the living prophets.

This personal revelation will surely come to all whose eyes are single to the glory of God, for it is promised that their bodies will be "filled with light, and there shall be no darkness" in them (D&C 88:67). Satan's efforts can be thwarted by all who come unto Christ by obedience to the covenants and ordinances of the gospel. The humble followers of the divine Master need not be deceived by the devil. Satan does not sustain and uplift and bless. He leaves those he has grasped in shame and misery. The Spirit of God is a sustaining and uplifting influence.

I emphasize that fasting and prayer are ways to receive the moral strength and spiritual strength to resist the temptations of Satan. But you may say this is hard and unpleasant. I commend to you the example of the Savior. He went into the desert, where he fasted and prayed to prepare himself spiritually for his ministry. His temptation by the devil was great, but through the purification of his spirit he was able to triumph over all evil.

Work is another deterrent to evil. The symbol of the state of Utah is the beehive. Our forefathers fostered industry and work. Elder John Longden quoted Herndon as saying: "Satan selects his disciples when they are idle; Jesus selected his when they were busy at their work either mending their nets or casting them into the sea."[19]

There are forces that will save us from the ever-increasing lying, disorder, violence, chaos, destruction, misery, and deceit that are now upon the earth. Those saving forces are the everlasting principles, covenants, and ordinances of the eternal gospel of the Lord Jesus Christ. These same principles, covenants, and ordinances are coupled with the rights and powers of the priesthood of Almighty God. We of this church are the possessors and custodians of these commanding powers, which can and do roll back much of the power of Satan on the earth. We believe that we hold these

"Let Your Light So Shine"

mighty forces in trust for all who have died, for all who are now living, and for those yet unborn.

Our challenge is to dedicate our lives to serving the Lord and not worry about offending the devil. Through the spreading of righteousness, the evil hands of the destroyer will be stayed, and he will not be permitted to curse the whole world. God will overlook our weaknesses, our frailties, and our many shortcomings and generously forgive us of our misdeeds as we repent and earnestly seek him.

Notes

1. Aurora Leigh, book VII.
2. William Shakespeare, *King Lear*, III, vi., 20.
3. *Gospel Doctrine* (Salt Lake City: Deseret Book Co., 1939), p. 373.
4. *Discourses of Brigham Young*, comp. John A. Widtsoe (Salt Lake City: Deseret Book Co., 1941), pp. 256–57.
5. Marion G. Romney, "The Price of Peace," address given at Brigham Young University, 1 March 1955.
6. Marion G. Romney, in Conference Report, October 1962, p. 94.
7. "Mother Teresa Has Anti-Abortion Answer," *The Salt Lake Tribune*, 15 February 1994, p. A11.
8. Ibid.
9. Ibid.
10. Ibid.
11. *Forbes Magazine*, 12 September 1994, p. 25.
12. "Ten Billion for Dinner, Please," *U.S. News and World Report*, 12 September 1994, pp. 57–60.
13. *The Screwtape Letters* (New York: Macmillan, 1961), pp. 64–65.
14. *Discourses of Brigham Young*, p. 410.
15. Howard W. Hunter, *Ensign*, November 1994, p. 8.
16. Delbert L. Stapley, in Conference Report, April 1958, p. 115.
17. *Teachings of the Prophet Joseph Smith*, p. 181.
18. *History of the Church*, 4:576.
19. John Longden, in Conference Report, April 1966, p. 39.

CHAPTER TEN

The Thankful Heart

T HE LORD HAS SAID, "And in nothing doth man offend God, or against none is his wrath kindled, save those who confess not his hand in all things, and obey not his commandments" (D&C 59:21). It is clear to me from this scripture that to "thank the Lord thy God in all things" (D&C 59:7) is more than a social courtesy; it is a binding commandment.

One of the advantages of having lived a long time is that you can often remember when you had it worse. I am grateful to have lived long enough to have known some of the blessings of adversity. My memory goes back to the Great Depression, when we had certain values burned into our souls. Because we had so little, one of these values we learned was gratitude for that which we had. The Great Depression in the United States in the early thirties was a terrible schoolmaster. We had to learn provident living in order to survive. Rather than create in us a spirit of envy or anger for what we did not have, it developed in many a spirit of gratitude for the meager, simple things with which we were blessed, like hot, homemade bread and oatmeal cereal and many other things.

As another example, I remember my beloved grandmother Mary Caroline Roper Finlinson making homemade soap on the farm. Her recipe for homemade soap included rendered animal fat, a small portion of lye as a cleansing agent, and wood ashes as an abrasive. The soap had a very pungent aroma and was almost as hard as a brick. There was no money to buy soft, sweet-smelling soap. On the farm, there were many dusty, sweat-laden clothes to be washed and many bodies that desperately needed a Saturday night bath. If you had to bathe with that homemade soap, you could become wonderfully clean, but you smelled worse after bathing than before. Since I use soap more now than I did as a child, I have developed a daily appreciation for mild, sweet-scented soap.

One of the evils of our time is taking for granted so many of the things we enjoy. This was spoken of by the Lord: "For what doth it profit a man if a gift is bestowed upon him, and he receive not the gift?" (D&C 88:33). The Apostle Paul described our day to Timothy when he wrote that in the last days "men shall be lovers of their own selves, covetous, boasters, proud, blasphemers, disobedient to parents, unthankful, unholy" (2 Timothy 3:2). These sins are fellow travelers, and ingratitude makes one susceptible to all of them.

The story of the thankful Samaritan has great meaning. As the Savior went through Samaria and Galilee, "he entered into a certain village, [and] there met him ten men that were lepers" and who "lifted up their voices and said, Jesus, Master, have mercy on us." Jesus told them to go show themselves unto the priest.

> And it came to pass, that, as they went, they were cleansed.
> And one of them, when he saw that he was healed, turned back, and with a loud voice glorified God.
> And fell down . . . at his feet, giving him thanks: and he was a Samaritan.
> And Jesus answering said, Were there not ten cleansed? but where are the nine?
> There are not found that returned to give glory to God, save this stranger.
> And he said unto him, Arise, go thy way: thy faith hath made thee whole. (Luke 17:11–19)

Leprosy was so loathsome a disease that those afflicted were not permitted under the law to come close to Jesus. Those suffer-

The Thankful Heart

ing from this terrible disease were required to agonize together, sharing their common misery (see Leviticus 13:45–46). Their forlorn cry, "Jesus, Master, have mercy on us" must have touched the Savior's heart. When they were healed and when they had received priestly approval that they were clean and acceptable in society, they must have been overcome with joy and amazement. Having received so great a miracle, they seemed completely satisfied. But they forgot their benefactor.

It is difficult to understand why the nine lepers were so lacking in gratitude. Such ingratitude is self-centered. It is a form of pride. What is the significance of the fact that the one who returned to give thanks was a Samaritan? As in the story of the good Samaritan, the point seems to be that those of lesser social or economic status often rise to a greater duty and nobility.

In addition to personal gratitude as a saving principle, I should like to express a feeling for the gratitude we ought to have for the many blessings we enjoy.

Those of you who have joined the Church in this generation have acquired fellowship with a people many of whom have a heritage of great suffering and sacrifice. Such sacrifice becomes your heritage also, for it is the inheritance of a people who have faults and imperfections but have a great nobility of purpose. That purpose is to help all mankind come to a sweet, peaceful understanding about who they are and to foster a love for their fellowmen and a determination to keep the commandments of God. This is the gospel's holy call. It is the essence of our worship.

Without question, we need to be informed of the happenings of the world. But modern communication brings into our homes a drowning cascade of the violence and misery of the worldwide human race. There comes a time when we need to find some peaceful spiritual renewal.

I acknowledge with great gratitude the peace and contentment we can find for ourselves in the spiritual cocoons of our homes, our sacrament meetings, and our holy temples. In these peaceful environments, our souls are rested. We have the feeling of having come home.

Some time ago, we were in the kingdom of Tonga. A family home evening, with music and spoken word, was arranged by President Muti in his stake center. The home evening was in honor of his majesty King Tupo the Fourth, the reigning monarch of Tonga. The king, his daughter, and his granddaughters graciously attended, as did many of the nobles and diplomatic representatives in Tonga. Our members put on a superb program of song and verse. One of the king's granddaughters sang a little solo entitled "How Much I Love My Grandfather." Elder John Sonnenberg and I were invited to respond briefly, which we were pleased to do.

After the program was over, the king ignored the usual royal protocol and came over to graciously greet us and our wives as an expression of appreciation for the performance of his subjects who are members of the Church. The thought came to me that social protocol is observed in many places, but the expression of kindness is universally appropriate.

It seems as though there is a tug-of-war between opposing character traits that leaves no voids in our souls. As gratitude is absent or disappears, rebellion often enters and fills the vacuum. I do not speak of rebellion against civil oppression. I refer to rebellion against moral cleanliness, beauty, decency, honesty, reverence, and respect for parental authority.

A grateful heart is a beginning of greatness. It is an expression of humility. It is a foundation for the development of such virtues as prayer, faith, courage, contentment, happiness, love, and well-being.

But there is a truism associated with all types of human strength: "Use it or lose it." When not used, muscles weaken, skills deteriorate, and faith disappears. President Thomas S. Monson stated: "Think to thank. In these three words are the finest capsule course for a happy marriage, a formula for enduring friendships, and a pattern for personal happiness."[1] Said the Lord, "And he who

The Thankful Heart

receiveth all things with thankfulness shall be made glorious; and the things of this earth shall be added unto him, even an hundred fold, yea, more" (D&C 78:19).

I am grateful for people on the earth who love and appreciate little children. One late night last year I found myself on an airplane bulging with passengers going north from Mexico City to Culiacán. The seats in the plane were close together, and every seat was taken, mostly by the gracious people of Mexico. Everywhere inside the plane there were packages and carry-on luggage of all sizes.

A young woman came down the aisle with four small children, the oldest of which appeared to be about four and the youngest a newborn. She was also trying to manage a diaper bag and a stroller and some bags. The tired children were crying and fussing. As she found her seat in the airplane, the passengers around her, both men and women, literally sprang to her aid. Soon the children were being lovingly and tenderly comforted and cared for by the passengers. They were passed from one passenger to another all over the airplane.

The result was an airplane full of baby-sitters. The children settled down in the caring arms of those who cradled them and, before long, went to sleep. Most remarkable was that a few men who were obviously fathers and grandfathers tenderly cradled and caressed the newborn child without any false, macho pride. The mother was freed from the care of her children most of the flight.

The only thing that I felt bad about was that no one passed the baby to me! I relearned that appreciation for and thoughtfulness and kindness to little children are an expression of the Savior's love for them.

How can we pay our debt of gratitude for the heritage of faith demonstrated by pioneers in many lands across the earth who struggled and sacrificed so that the gospel might take root? How is thankfulness expressed for the intrepid handcart pioneers who, by their own brute strength, pulled their meager belongings in handcarts across the scorching plains and through the snows of the high mountain passes to escape persecution and find peaceful worship in these valleys? How can the debt of gratitude possibly be paid by the descendants of the Martin and the Willie and the other hand-cart companies for the faith of their forebears?

One of these intrepid souls was Emma Batchelor, a young English girl traveling without family. She started out with the Willie Handcart Company, but by the time they reached Fort Laramie, they were ordered to lighten their loads. Emma was directed to leave the copper kettle in which she carried all of her belongings.

She refused to do this and set it by the side of the road and sat down on it. She knew that the Martin Handcart Company was only a few days behind. So although she had been privileged to start with the Willie company, when the Martin company caught up, she joined the Paul Gourley family.

A young son wrote many years later: "Here we were joined by Sister Emma Batchelor. We were glad to have her because she was young and strong and meant more flour for our mess." It was here that Sister Gourley gave birth to a child, and Emma acted as the midwife and loaded the mother and the child in the cart for two days, then helped pull the cart.

Those who died in the Martin company were mercifully relieved of the suffering others endured—frozen feet, ears, noses, or fingers—which maimed them for the rest of their lives. However, Emma, age twenty-one, was a fortunate one. She came through the ordeal whole.

A year later, she met Brigham Young, who was surprised that she was not maimed, and she told him, "Brother Brigham, I had no one to care for me or to look out for me, so I decided I must look out for myself. I was the one who called out when Brother Savage warned us [not to go]. I was at fault in that, but I tried to make up for it. I pulled my share at the cart every day. When we came to a stream, I stopped and took off my shoes and stockings and outer skirt and put them on top of the cart. Then, after I got the cart across, I came back and carried little Paul over on my back. Then I

The Thankful Heart

sat down and scrubbed my feet hard with my woolen neckerchief and put on dry shoes and stockings."

The descendants of these pioneers can partially settle the account by being true to the cause for which their ancestors suffered so much.

As with all commandments, gratitude is a description of a successful mode of living. The thankful heart opens our eyes to a multitude of blessings that continually surround us. President J. Reuben Clark Jr. said, "Hold fast to the blessings which God has provided for you. Yours is not the task to gain them, they are here; yours is the part of cherishing them."[2] I hope that we may cultivate grateful hearts so that we may cherish the multitude of blessings that God has so graciously bestowed. May we openly express such gratitude to our Heavenly Father and our fellowmen.

NOTES

1. *Pathways to Perfection* (Salt Lake City: Deseret Book Co., 1973), p. 254.
2. *Church News,* 14 June 1969, p. 2.

PART THREE

"Bring Up Your Children in Light and Truth"
Parents, Priesthood, and Children

CHAPTER ELEVEN

A Thousand Threads of Love

PARENTHOOD IS THE greatest challenge in the world. In fact, on the subject of parenthood there are about as many opinions as there are parents, yet there are few who claim to have all of the answers. I am certainly not one of them.

I feel that there are more outstanding young men and women among our people at present than at any other moment in my lifetime. This presupposes that most of these fine young people have come from good homes and are blessed with committed, caring parents. Even so, the most conscientious parents feel that they may have made some mistakes. One time, when I did a thoughtless thing, I remember my own mother exclaiming, "Where did I fail?"

The Lord has directed, "Bring up your children in light and truth" (D&C 93:40). To me, there is no more important human effort. Being a father or a mother is not only a great challenge, it is a divine calling. It is an effort requiring consecration. President David O. McKay stated that being parents is "the greatest trust" that has been given to human beings.[1]

While few human challenges are greater than that of being good parents, few opportunities offer greater potential for joy. Surely no more important work is to be done in this world than preparing our children to be God-fearing, happy, honorable, and productive adults. Parents will find no more fulfilling happiness than to have their children honor them and their teachings. That blessing is the glory of parenthood. John testified, "I have no greater joy than to hear that my children walk in truth" (3 John 1:4).

In my opinion, the teaching, rearing, and training of children requires more intelligence, intuitive understanding, humility, strength, wisdom, spirituality, perseverance, and hard work than any other challenge we might have in life. This is especially so when moral foundations of honor and decency are eroding around us. If we are to have successful homes, values must be taught. There must be rules, there must be standards, and there must be absolutes. Many societies give parents very little support in teaching and honoring moral values. A number of cultures are becoming essentially valueless, and many of the younger people in those societies are becoming moral cynics.

As societies as a whole have decayed and lost their moral identity and as so many homes are broken, the best hope is to turn greater attention and effort to the teaching of the next generation—our children. In order to do this, we must first reinforce the primary teachers of children. Chief among these are the parents and other family members, and the best environment for this teaching should be the home. Somehow, some way, we must try harder to make our homes stronger so that they will stand as sanctuaries against the unwholesome, pervasive moral dry rot around us. Harmony, happiness, peace, and love in the home can help give children the required inner strength to cope with life's challenges. Barbara Bush, wife of former U.S. President George Bush, once said to the graduates of Wellesley College:

"Whatever the era, whatever the times, one thing will never change: Fathers and mothers, if you have children, they must come first. You must read to your children and you must hug your children and you must love your children. Your success as a family, our success as a society, depends not on what happens in the White House but on what happens inside your house."[2]

To be a good father and mother requires that the parents defer many of their own needs and desires in favor of the needs of their children. As a consequence of this sacrifice, conscientious parents develop a nobility of character and learn to put into practice the selfless truths taught by the Savior himself.

I have the greatest respect for single parents who struggle and sacrifice, trying against almost impossible odds to hold the family together. They should be honored and helped in their heroic efforts. But any mother's or father's task is much easier where there are two functioning parents in the home. Children often challenge and tax the strength and wisdom of both parents.

A few years ago, Bishop Stanley Smoot was interviewed by President Spencer W. Kimball. President Kimball asked, "How often do you have family prayer?"

Bishop Smoot answered, "We try to have family prayer twice a day, but we average about once."

President Kimball answered, "In the past, having family prayer once a day may have been all right. But in the future it will not be enough if we are going to save our families."

I wonder if having casual and infrequent family home evenings will be enough in the future to fortify our children with sufficient moral strength. In the future, infrequent family scripture study may be inadequate to arm our children with the virtue necessary to withstand the moral decay of the environment in which they will live. Where in the world will the children learn chastity, integrity, honesty, and basic human decency if not at home? These values will, of course, be reinforced at church, but parental teaching is more constant.

When parents try to teach their children to avoid danger, it is no answer for parents to say to their children, "We are experienced and wise in the ways of the world, and therefore we can get closer to the edge of the cliff than you." Parental hypocrisy can make children cynical and unbelieving of what they are taught in the home. For instance, when parents attend movies they forbid their children to see, parental credibility is diminished. If children are expected to be honest, parents must be honest. If children are expected to be virtuous, parents must be virtuous. If you expect your children to be honorable, you must be honorable.

Among the other values children should be taught are respect for others (beginning with the child's own parents and family), respect for the symbols of faith and the patriotic beliefs of others, respect for law and order, respect for the property of others, and respect for authority. Paul reminds us that children should "learn first to shew piety at home" (1 Timothy 5:4).

One of the most difficult parental challenges is to appropriately discipline children. Child rearing is so individualistic. Every child is different and unique. What works with one may not work with another. I do not know who is wise enough to say what discipline is too harsh or what is too lenient except the parents of the children themselves, who love them most. It is a matter of prayerful discernment for the parents. Certainly the overarching and undergirding principle is that the discipline of children must be motivated more by love than by punishment. President Brigham Young counseled, "If you are ever called upon to chasten a person, never chasten beyond the balm you have within you to bind up."[3] Direction and discipline are, however, certainly an indispensable part of child rearing. If parents do not discipline their children, then the public will discipline them in a way the parents do not like. Without discipline, children will not respect the rules of either the home or society.

A principal purpose for discipline is to teach obedience. President David O. McKay stated, "Parents who fail to teach obedience to their children, if [their] homes do not develop obedience society will demand it and get it. It is therefore better for the home, with its kindliness, sympathy and understanding to train the child in obedience rather than callously to leave him to the brutal and unsympathetic discipline that society will impose if the home has not already fulfilled its obligation."[4]

An essential part of teaching children to be disciplined and responsible is to have them learn to work. As we grow up, many of

A Thousand Threads of Love

us are like the man who said, "I like work; it fascinates me. I can sit and look at it for hours."[5] Again, the best teachers of the principle of work are the parents themselves. For me, work became a joy when I first worked alongside my father, grandfather, uncles, and brothers. I am sure that I was often more of an aggravation than a help, but the memories are sweet and the lessons learned are valuable. Children need to learn responsibility and independence. Are the parents personally taking the time to show and demonstrate and explain so that children can, as Lehi taught, "act for themselves and not . . . be acted upon"? (2 Nephi 2:26).

Luther Burbank, one of the world's greatest horticulturists, said, "If we had paid no more attention to our plants than we have to our children, we would now be living in a jungle of weeds."[6]

Children are also beneficiaries of moral agency by which we are all afforded the opportunity to progress, grow, and develop. That agency also permits children to pursue the alternate choices of selfishness, wastefulness, self-indulgence, and self-destruction. Children often express this agency when very young.

Let parents who have been conscientious, loving, and concerned and who have lived the principles of righteousness as best they could be comforted in knowing that they are good parents despite the actions of some of their children. The children themselves have a responsibility to listen, obey, and, having been taught, to learn. Parents cannot always answer for all their children's misconduct, because even the most diligent parents cannot ensure their children's good behavior. Some few children could tax even Solomon's wisdom and Job's patience.

There is often a special challenge for those parents who are affluent or overly indulgent. In a sense, some children in those circumstances hold their parents hostage by withholding their support of parental rules unless the parents acquiesce to the children's demands. Elder Neal A. Maxwell of the Quorum of the Twelve has said, "Those who do too much *for* their children will soon find they can do nothing *with* their children. So many children have been so much *done for* they are almost *done in*."[7] It seems to be human nature that we do not fully appreciate material things we have not ourselves earned.

There is a certain irony in the fact that some parents are so anxious for their children to be accepted by and be popular with their peers; yet these same parents fear that their children may be doing the things their peers are doing.

Generally, those children who make the decision and have the resolve to abstain from drugs, alcohol, and illicit sex are those who have adopted and internalized the strong values of their homes as lived by their parents. In times of difficult decisions they are most likely to follow the teaching of their parents rather than the example of their peers or the sophistries of the media, which glamorize alcohol consumption, illicit sex, infidelity, dishonesty, and other vices. Those young people who demonstrate moral courage are like Helaman's two thousand young men who "had been taught by their mothers, that if they did not doubt, God would deliver them" from death (Alma 56:47). "And they rehearsed . . . the words of their mothers, saying: We do not doubt our mothers knew it" (verse 48).

What seems to help cement parental teachings and values in place in children's lives is a firm belief in Deity. When this belief becomes part of children's very souls, they have inner strength. So, of all that is important to be taught, what should parents teach? The scriptures tell us that parents are to teach their children "faith in Christ the Son of the living God, and of baptism and the gift of the Holy Ghost," as well as "the doctrine of repentance" (D&C 68:25). These truths must be taught in the home. They cannot be taught in the public schools, nor will they be fostered by the government or society. Of course, Church programs can help, but the most effective teaching takes place in the home.

Parental teaching moments need not be big or dramatic or powerful. We learn this from the Master Teacher. Commenting on the Savior, one writer said:

A Thousand Threads of Love

The completed beauty of Christ's life is only the added beauty of little inconspicuous acts of beauty—talking with the woman at the well; . . . showing the young ruler the stealthy ambition laid away in his heart that kept him out of the kingdom of Heaven; . . . teaching a little knot of followers how to pray; . . . kindling a fire and broiling fish that his disciples might have a breakfast waiting for them when they came ashore from a night of fishing, cold, tired, and discouraged. All of these things, you see, let us in so easily into the real quality and tone of [Christ's] interests, so specific, so narrowed down, so enlisted in what is small, so engrossed with what is minute.[8]

And so it is with being parents. The little things are the big things sewn into the family tapestry by a thousand threads of love, faith, discipline, sacrifice, patience, and work.

There are some great spiritual promises that parents may have visited upon them; these are the same divine promises made to their valiant forbears who nobly kept their covenants. Covenants remembered by parents will be remembered by God. The children may thus become the beneficiaries and inheritors of these great covenants and promises. This is because they are the children of the covenant.[9]

God bless the struggling, sacrificing, honorable parents of this world. May he especially honor the covenants kept by faithful parents among our people, and may he watch over these children of the covenant.

NOTES

1. *The Responsibility of Parents to Their Children,* pamphlet (Salt Lake City: The Church of Jesus Christ of Latter-day Saints, n.d.), p. 1.

2. *Washington Post,* 2 June 1990, p. 2.

3. In *Journal of Discourses,* 9:124–25.

4. *The Responsibility of Parents to Their Children,* p. 3.

5. Jerome Klapka Jerome, as quoted in *The International Dictionary of Thoughts,* comp. John P. Bradley, Leo F. Daniels, and Thomas C. Jones (Chicago: J.G. Ferguson Publishing Co., 1969), p. 782.

"Bring Up Your Children in Light and Truth"

6. As quoted in *Elbert Hubbard's Scrap Book* (New York: Wm. H. Wise and Co., 1923), p. 227.

7. In Conference Report, Apr. 1975, p. 150; or *Ensign,* May 1975, p. 101.

8. Charles Henry Parkhurst, "Kindness and Love," in *Leaves of Gold* (Honesdale, Pa.: Coslet Publishing Co., 1938), p. 177.

9. See Orson F. Whitney, in Conference Report, Apr. 1929, pp. 110–11.

CHAPTER TWELVE

Youth, Listen to the Voice of the Spirit

I AM WELL AWARE that the world in which the youth of today live will be vastly different from the one I have known. Values have changed. Basic decency and respect for good things are eroding. A moral blackness is settling in. You young people are in many ways the hope of the future, and I remind you that valuable diamonds shine better against a dark background.

For you outstanding young men and women there is a scriptural text found in the Doctrine and Covenants: "Give ear to the voice of the living God" (D&C 50:1). The voice of the Spirit is universally available to all. The Lord said, "The Spirit enlighteneth every man [and every woman] . . . that hearkeneth to the voice of the Spirit" (D&C 84:46). He further says that "every one that hearkeneth to the voice of the Spirit cometh unto God, even the Father" (D&C 84:47). Some people are seeking to find the abundant life. The apostle Paul made it clear that it is "the spirit [that] giveth life" (2 Corinthians 3:6). Indeed, the Savior said, "The words that I speak unto you, they are spirit, and they are life" (John 6:63).

You may ask, "Then what are the fruits of the Spirit?" Paul answered this by saying they are "love, joy, peace, longsuffering, gentleness, goodness, faith, meekness, temperance" (Galatians 5:22–23). The joy we seek is not a temporary emotional high but a habitual inner joy learned from long experience and trust in God. Ralph Waldo Emerson wrote, "Rectitude is a perpetual victory,

"Bring Up Your Children in Light and Truth"

celebrated not by cries of joy, but by serenity, which is joy fixed or habitual."[1]

Lehi taught his firstborn son, Jacob, "Men are, that they might have joy" (2 Nephi 2:25). To achieve this great objective, we must "give ear to the voice of the living God" (D&C 50:1).

I wish to testify as a living witness that joy does come through listening to the spirit, for I have experienced it. Those who live the gospel learn to live "after the manner of happiness," as did the Nephites (see 2 Nephi 5:27). All over the world, in the many countries where the Church is established, members could add their testimonies to mine. Abundant evidence verifies the promise of peace, hope, love, and joy as gifts of the spirit. Our voices join in a united petition for all of God's children to partake of these gifts also.

But we hear other voices. Paul said, "There are . . . so many kinds of voices in the world" (1 Corinthians 14:10) that compete with the voice of the Spirit. Let's suppose that you are trying at this moment to hear just one voice, my voice as I testify of the truths of the gospel. Imagine, however, what would happen if all of a sudden, as you were reading these words, a heckler started to yell obscenities nearby; another began to contend with him; another began to debate with his neighbor; and someone else turned on a recording of some loud music. Soon a chorus of raucous, rival voices would smother my voice, and it would be difficult, if not impossible, for you to receive my intended spiritual message.

Such is the situation in the world. The Spirit's voice is ever-present, but it is calm. Said Isaiah, "And the work of righteousness shall be peace; and the effect of righteousness quietness and assurance for ever" (Isaiah 32:17). The adversary tries to smother this voice with a multitude of loud, persistent, persuasive, and appealing voices:

- Murmuring voices that conjure up perceived injustices.
- Whining voices that abhor challenge and work.
- Seductive voices offering sensual enticements.
- Soothing voices that lull us into carnal security.

Youth, Listen to the Voice of the Spirit

- Intellectual voices that profess sophistication and scholarly superiority.
- Proud voices that rely on the arm of flesh.
- Flattering voices that puff us up with pride.
- Cynical voices that destroy hope.
- Entertaining voices that promote pleasure seeking.
- Commercial voices that tempt us to "spend money for that which is of no worth" and to "labor for that which cannot satisfy" (2 Nephi 9:51).
- Delirious voices that spawn the desire for a "high." I refer not to a drug- or alcohol-induced high but rather a high obtained by pursuing dangerous, death-defying experiences for nothing more than a thrill. Life, even our own, is so precious that we are accountable to the Lord for it, and we should not trifle with it. Once gone, it cannot be called back. There are so many manifestations of this foolhardy thrill seeking that I will not enumerate them for fear of giving someone an idea. "The knowledge of sin tempteth to its commission."[2]

In your generation you will be barraged by multitudes of voices telling you how to live, how to gratify your passions, how to have it all. You will have up to five hundred television channels at your fingertips. There will be all sorts of software, interactive computer modems, databases, and bulletin boards; there will be desktop publishing, satellite receivers, and communications networks that will suffocate you with information. Local cable news networks will cover only local news. Everyone will be under more scrutiny. There will be fewer places of refuge and serenity. You will be bombarded with evil and wickedness like no other generation. As I contemplate this prospect, I am reminded of T. S. Eliot's words, "Where is the wisdom we have lost in knowledge? Where is the knowledge we have lost in information?"[3]

Without question some will be deceived and will endure lives of heartbreak and sadness. Others will enjoy the promise recorded by Jeremiah, "I will put my law in their inward parts" (Jeremiah 31:33). In some ways it will be harder to be faithful in your day, perhaps in some ways even more challenging than pulling a handcart across the plains. When someone died in the wilderness of frontier America, their physical remains were buried and the handcarts continued west, but the mourning survivors had hope for their loved one's eternal soul. However, when someone dies spiritually in the wilderness of sin, hope may be replaced by dread and fear for the loved one's eternal welfare.

Many in your generation have been conditioned by the world to want it all and to want it now. Many do not want to save or work. Such self-centered, impatient desires make you susceptible to temptation. The Book of Mormon identifies four categories of enticements that Satan appeals to: getting gain, relying on the power of the flesh, seeking popularity, and seeking the lusts of the flesh and the things of the world (see 1 Nephi 22:23).

Satan's tactic is to "turn their hearts away from the truth, that they become blinded and understand not the things which are prepared for them" (D&C 78:10). He creates a smoke screen that obscures our vision and diverts our attention.

President Heber J. Grant stated: "If we are faithful in keeping the commandments of God His promises will be fulfilled to the very letter. . . . The trouble is, the adversary of men's souls blinds their minds. He throws dust, so to speak, in their eyes, and they are blinded with the things of this world."[4]

How are you possibly going to select what voices you will listen to and believe? The implications for you as individuals are staggering. To survive, you must learn to follow the voice of the Spirit. You learn this as you live the gospel. There are specific aspects of the gospel that, if you focus carefully on them, will help you as you listen for the voice of the Spirit.

First, exercise your moral agency wisely. Omni tells us how we can make the proper channel selections. "There is nothing which is good save it comes from the Lord; and that which is evil cometh from the devil" (Omni 1:25). Every moment demands that we choose, over and over again, between that which comes from the Lord and that which comes from the devil. As tiny drops of water shape a landscape, so our minute-by-minute choices shape our character. Living the eternal gospel every day may be harder than dying for the Church and the Lord.

Moroni also contrasts those things that "inviteth and enticeth to sin" with those that "inviteth and enticeth to do good continually" (Moroni 7:12–13). He gives the key for judging:

"Seeing that ye know the light by which ye may judge, which light is the light of Christ, see that ye do not judge wrongfully;

"Wherefore, I beseech of you, brethren, that ye should search diligently in the light of Christ that ye may know good from evil; and if ye will lay hold upon every good thing, and condemn it not, ye certainly will be a child of Christ" (Moroni 7:18–19).

You will not be able to travel through life on borrowed light. The light of life must be part of your very being. The voice you must learn to heed is the voice of the Spirit.

Second, you must have a purpose. In December 1992 when we were in Israel with the Tabernacle Choir, the leaders of the choir, Brother Truman Madsen, and I were honored to have an interview with Mr. Shimon Perez, foreign secretary of Israel and former prime minister. He told us a story I shall never forget. He said that as a young boy he rode in a car from Tel Aviv to Haifa in the Holy Land with David Ben-Gurion, the George Washington of the state of Israel. On the way up, without any explanation, President Ben-Gurion said, "Trotsky was no leader." He was referring to Leon Trotsky, one of the architects of the Russian communist revolution. A little while later he added, "Trotsky was brilliant, but he was no leader because he had no purpose."

Everyone in life needs to have a purpose. As members of Christ's church, we are to consider the end of our salvation (see D&C 46:7). Someone has said, "You must stand up for something or you will fall for everything."

"If your eye be single to my glory, your whole bodies shall be filled with light, and there shall be no darkness in you" (D&C 88:67).

"A double minded man is unstable in all his ways" (James 1:8).

"Let the mind be concentrated, and it possesses almighty power. It is the agent of the Almighty clothed with mortal tabernacles, and we must learn to discipline it, and bring it to bear on one point."⁵

The more righteous part of the Nephites had to learn to focus attention in order to hear the voice. "They heard a voice as if it came out of heaven; and they cast their eyes round about, for they understood not the voice which they heard; and it was not a harsh voice, neither was it a loud voice; nevertheless, and notwithstanding it being a small voice it did pierce them that did hear to the center, insomuch that there was no part of their frame that it did not cause to quake; yea, it did pierce them to the very soul, and did cause their hearts to burn" (3 Nephi 11:3). They heard a voice a second time, and did not understand. When they heard the voice the third time, they "did open their ears to hear it; and their eyes were towards the sound thereof; and they did look steadfastly towards heaven, from whence the sound came" (verses 4–5). If we are to hearken to the voice of the Spirit, we too must open our ears, turn the eye of faith to the source of the voice, and look steadfastly toward heaven.

Be aware that there are invisible hosts watching over you even as they did Elisha of old. The King of Syria sent hosts of warriors with chariots and horses to capture the prophet Elisha. They came by night and surrounded the city. Elisha's servants, seeing the great hosts, became very frightened and said to Elisha, "Alas, my master, how shall we do?"

"And Elisha prayed, and said, Lord, I pray thee, open his eyes, that he may see. And the Lord opened the eyes of the young man; and he saw: and, behold, the mountain was full of horses and chariots of fire about Elisha."

In answer to his servant's frightened question, Elisha said, "Fear not: for they that be with us are more than they that be with them" (2 Kings 6:15–17).

My dear young friends, I believe that unseen spiritual hosts tend you as you seek to do the will of the Lord. Remember the words of Elisha: "They that be with us are more than they that be with them" (verse 16).

Third, strengthen your testimony. Everyone in life needs to have spiritual goals. One way to learn of our life's purpose is to have our patriarchal blessings. A choice young man recently received his patriarchal blessing. He was told in his blessing that many of his forebears who had paid a terrible price for the gospel were present as the blessing was given. Your patriarchal blessing is one important way to learn of your life's purpose.

If I were to ask you young people, "How is your testimony?" I suppose that many of you would say, "I don't know." But if I asked you some specific questions, the result would be different. For instance, if I asked you, "Do you believe that God lives and that we are his children?" I think most of you would answer this question quickly and affirmatively.

And if I asked, "Do you believe and have faith in the Lord Jesus Christ as our Savior and Redeemer?" I think most of you would hasten to say yes.

And if I then asked, "Do you believe that Joseph Smith was the prophet of the Restoration?" I think most of you would agree that you believe this. Some of you would already be familiar with section 135 of the Doctrine and Covenants, which states that "Joseph Smith, the Prophet and Seer of the Lord, has done more, save Jesus only, for the salvation of men in this world, than any other man that ever lived in it" (D&C 135:3).

If I were to ask you, "Do you believe the Book of Mormon is the word of God?" I think many of you would agree that you have already acquired a testimony concerning the truthfulness of the Book of Mormon.

"Bring Up Your Children in Light and Truth"

Lastly, if I were to ask you, "Do you believe that President Gordon B. Hinckley and his counselors and the members of the Quorum of the Twelve Apostles are the prophets, seers, and revelators of our day?" I think most of you would answer that you have formed a respect for the leaders of this church.

Having answered these five questions in the affirmative, you already have a foundation of a testimony. As you acquire knowledge of the plan of salvation and learn why you are here and where you are going, your testimony will be strengthened. You of this generation are a chosen generation. You are walking on the path to testimony and strength; your task now is to continue progressing along that path.

You young women have a great destiny. As part of this destiny, you have a precious work to do. President Spencer W. Kimball wrote: "It is a great blessing to be a woman in the Church today. The opposition against righteousness has never been greater, but the opportunities for fulfilling our highest potential have also never been greater."[6] Women are so richly endowed with the spiritual gifts about which Paul spoke: faith, hope, and charity (see 1 Corinthians 13:13). Thus, part of your destiny is to set the example of the sublime womanly virtues while you serve as the nurturers, the teachers, and the refining influence so important for our families and the Church. Women are the enriching adornment of the race.

Learn and gain a testimony of the plan of salvation. "God gave unto them commandments, after having made known unto them the plan of redemption, that they should not do evil" (Alma 12:32). Learn of your relationship to God. As you walk by faith, you will have confirmed in your young hearts spiritual experiences that will strengthen your faith and testimony.

Fourth, search the scriptures, which are "the voice of the Lord, and the power of God unto salvation" (D&C 68:4). The Lord also said of his word, as found in the scriptures, that "it is my voice which speaketh them unto you; for they are given by my Spirit unto you, and by my power you can read them one to another; . . .

wherefore, you can testify that you have heard my voice, and know my words" (D&C 18:35–36).

Fifth, gain a conviction of the divine calling of the Brethren and be willing to follow their counsel, including the following important principles:

Honor the priesthood. You young men are part of a royal priesthood. You young men and women were, no doubt, chosen before the world was and reserved to come forward in this time. We love you. We have confidence in you. We know that you will be equal to the challenges that are placed before you to carry forward the work of the Lord as your parents and grandparents and forebears have done. We know it is hard. You live in a morally desensitizing environment, but you must always remember that someone is listening and watching. If you support and sustain the priesthood, that power will be a great stabilizing influence in your lives.

Stay morally clean. You must believe that it is worth it in the end to be true and faithful. Worldly pleasures do not match up to heavenly joy. It may not be "cool" to avoid certain things, or "rad" to do other things, but it is better to be alone and to be right than to be eternally wrong. We counsel you to associate with those who can help you maintain your standards rather than tear them down. You must learn to be your own person and to live by your own standards. Even though you may have become somewhat desensitized or may have made some mistakes, you must not let Satan reduce your self-esteem to the point that you become discouraged from righteous living. We urge you to carry and frequently read your *For the Strength of Youth* booklet and to listen to your parents and your leaders. Because you are a chosen generation, there is not a problem that you cannot handle with the help of the Lord. We counsel you not to grow up too fast. Do not miss the joy of being a righteous young adult. Enjoy your dating years. Have many friends. Have confidence in yourselves and in your future. You must learn to labor, and you must learn to wait.

I warn you of a pervasive false doctrine. For want of a better name, I call it "premeditated repentance," by which I mean consciously sinning with the forethought that afterward repentance will permit the enjoyment of the full blessings of the gospel, such as temple marriage or a mission. In an increasingly wicked society, it is harder to toy with evil without becoming contaminated. This foolish doctrine was foreseen by Nephi:

"And there shall also be many which shall say: Eat, drink, and be merry; nevertheless, fear God—he will justify in committing a little sin; yea, lie a little, take the advantage of one because of his words, dig a pit for thy neighbor; there is no harm in this; and do all these things, for tomorrow we die; and if it so be that we are guilty, God will beat us with a few stripes, and at last we shall be saved in the kingdom of God" (2 Nephi 28:8).

Of all those who teach this doctrine, the Lord says, "The blood of the saints shall cry from the ground against them" (verse 10).

Lastly, I do not know how the Lord will discipline your generation because of the general callousness and hardness of the hearts of so many in society. In Biblical times the Lord sent fiery, flying serpents among the people. After the people were bitten by the serpents, the Lord prepared a way for them to be healed. As commanded by the Lord, Moses made a serpent of brass and put it on a pole. To be healed, those who were bitten had only to look upon the brass serpent (see Numbers 21:8–9). This was too simple for many, and "because of the simpleness of the way, or the easiness of it, there were many who perished" (1 Nephi 17:41).

I have suggested a simple solution for selecting the channel to which you will attune yourselves: Listen to and follow the voice of the Spirit. This is an ancient solution, even eternal, and may not be popular in a society that is always looking for something new. This solution requires patience in a world that demands instant gratification. This solution is quiet, peaceful, and subtle in a world enamored by that which is loud, incessant, fast-paced, garish, and crude. This solution requires you to be contemplative while your peers seek physical titillation.

Youth, Listen to the Voice of the Spirit

If you are to accept this solution of listening to and following the voice of the Spirit, you must allow the prophets to "put you always in remembrance of these things, though ye know them, and be established in the present truth" (2 Peter 1:12). This may seem too foolish and simple a solution in a time when it is not worth remembering much of the trivial tripe to which we are exposed.

The solution of listening to and following the voice of the Spirit is one unified, consistent, age-old message in a world that quickly becomes bored in the absence of intensity, variety, and novelty.

This solution requires you to walk by faith in a world governed by sight (see 2 Corinthians 4:18; 5:7). You must see with the eye of faith eternal, unseen, spiritual verities while the masses of mankind depend solely on temporal things, which can be known only through the physical senses.

In short, this solution may not be popular, and it may not get you gain or worldly power. But "our light affliction, which is but for a moment, worketh for us a far more exceeding and eternal weight of glory" (2 Corinthians 4:17).

Learn to ponder the things of the Spirit and to respond to its promptings; filter out the static generated by Satan. As you become attuned to the Spirit, "thine ears shall hear a word behind thee, saying, This is the way, walk ye in it" (Isaiah 30:21). Hearkening to the "voice of the living God" will give you "peace in this world, and eternal life in the world to come" (D&C 59:23). These are the greatest of all the gifts of God (see D&C 14:7).

I pray with Paul "unto the Father of our Lord Jesus Christ . . . that he would grant you, according to the riches of his glory, to be strengthened with might by his Spirit in the inner man; that Christ may dwell in your hearts by faith; that ye, being rooted and grounded in love, may . . . know the love of Christ, which passeth knowledge, that ye might be filled with all the fulness of God" (Ephesians 3:14–19).

I believe and testify that your spirits are special spirits and were reserved until this generation to stand strong against the evil winds that blow and to stand straight and upright with the heavy burdens that will be placed upon you. I am confident you will be faithful and true to the great trust placed in you and the great work ahead of you.

NOTES

1. "Character," *Emerson: Essays and Lectures,* p. 500.

2. Joseph F. Smith, *Gospel Doctrine* (Salt Lake City: Deseret Book Co., 1939), p. 373.

3. "Choruses from 'The Rock,'" *The Complete Poems and Plays* (New York: Harcourt, Brace & World, Inc., 1930), p. 96.

4. Heber J. Grant, *Gospel Standards* (Salt Lake City: Deseret Book Co., 1969), pp. 44–45.

5. Orson Hyde, in *Journal of Discourses,* 7:152–53.

6. As quoted in G. Homer Durham, "Woman's Responsibility to Learn," in *Woman* (Salt Lake City: Deseret Book Co., 1979), p. 33.

CHAPTER THIRTEEN

Keeping the Sabbath Day Holy

I CONFESS THAT WHEN I was a young boy, Sunday was not my favorite day. Grandfather shut down the action. We didn't have any transportation. We couldn't drive the car. He wouldn't even let us start the motor. We couldn't ride the horses or the steers or the sheep. It was the Sabbath, and by commandment the animals also needed rest. We walked to church and everywhere else we wanted to go. I can honestly say that we observed both the spirit and the letter of Sabbath worship.

By today's standards, perhaps Grandfather's interpretation of Sabbath day activities seems extreme, but something wonderful has been lost in our lives. To this day, I have been pondering to try to understand fully what has slipped away. Part of it was knowing that because of my strict observance of the Sabbath, I was well on the Lord's side of the line. Another part was the feeling that Satan's influence was further away on the Sabbath. Mostly it was the reinforcement received by the spiritual power which was generated. We had the rich feeling that the spiritual "fulness of the earth" (D&C 59:16) was ours, as promised by the Lord in section 59 of the Doctrine and Covenants. I have observed that, unfortunately, many in our generation are missing great blessings by not honoring the Lord's day.

Ever since Adam's day, the divine law of the Sabbath has been emphasized repeatedly over the centuries, perhaps more than any other commandment. This long emphasis alone is an indication of the importance of the commandment. In Genesis we learn that God himself set the example for us in the creation of the earth:

> Thus the heavens and the earth were finished, and all the host of them.
> And on the seventh day God ended his work which he had made; and he rested on the seventh day from all his work which he had made.
> And God blessed the seventh day, and sanctified it: because that in it he had rested from all his work which God created and made. (Genesis 2:1–3)

In biblical times this commandment to rest and worship was so strict that a violation of it called for the death penalty (see Exodus 31:15). Even the earth was given a sabbath rest: "But in the seventh year shall be a sabbath of rest unto the land, a sabbath for the Lord: thou shalt neither sow thy field, nor prune thy vineyard" (Leviticus 25:4).

The Sabbath was referred to in the Old Testament days as a blessed and hallowed day (see Exodus 20:11), as a symbol of a perpetual covenant of faithfulness (see Exodus 31:16), as a holy convocation (see Leviticus 23:3), and as a day of spiritual celebration (see Leviticus 23:32).

Jesus reaffirmed the importance of the Sabbath day devotion, but he introduced a new spirit into this part of worship. Rather than observe the endless technicalities and prohibitions concerning what should and should not be done on the Lord's day, he affirmed that it is lawful to do well on the Sabbath (see Matthew 12:12). He taught us that "the Son of man is Lord even of the sabbath day" (verse 8) and introduced the principle that "the sabbath was made for man, and not man for the sabbath" (Mark 2:27). He performed good deeds on the Sabbath, such as healing the man with palsy (see Mark 2:1–12) as well as the man with the paralyzed hand (see Matthew 12:10–13). So the divine mandate of Sabbath day observance in our day is now a manifestation of individual devotion and commitment rather than a requirement of civil law.

The great modern-day revelation on Sabbath day worship is contained in section 59 of the Doctrine and Covenants:

> And that thou mayest more fully keep thyself unspotted from the world, thou shalt go to the house of prayer and offer up thy sacraments upon my holy day;
>
> For verily this is a day appointed unto you to rest from your labors, and to pay thy devotions unto the Most High;
>
> Nevertheless thy vows shall be offered up in righteousness on all days and at all times;
>
> But remember that on this, the Lord's day, thou shalt offer thine oblations and thy sacraments unto the Most High, confessing thy sins unto thy brethren, and before the Lord.
>
> And on this day thou shalt do none other thing, only let thy food be prepared with singleness of heart that thy fasting may be perfect, or, in other words, that thy joy may be full. (D&C 59:9–13)

This great commandment concludes with a promise: "Verily I say, that inasmuch as ye do this, the fulness of the earth is yours, the beasts of the field and the fowls of the air, and that which climbeth upon the trees and walketh upon the earth" (verse 16). To have the benefit of all of God's creations is a very significant promise.

Keeping the Sabbath day holy is much more than just physical rest. It involves spiritual renewal and worship. President Spencer W. Kimball gave excellent counsel on Sabbath day observance. He said:

> The Sabbath is a holy day in which to do worthy and holy things. Abstinence from work and recreation is important but insufficient. The Sabbath calls for constructive thoughts and acts, and if one merely lounges about doing nothing on the Sabbath, he is breaking it. To observe it, one will be on his knees in prayer, preparing lessons, studying

"Bring Up Your Children in Light and Truth"

the gospel, meditating, visiting the ill and distressed, sleeping, reading wholesome material, and attending all the meetings of that day to which he is expected. To fail to do these proper things is a transgression on the omission side.[1]

Over a lifetime of observation, I have noticed that the farmer who observes the Sabbath day seems to get more done on his farm than he would if he worked seven days. The mechanic will be able to turn out more and better products in six days than in seven. The doctor, the lawyer, the dentist, or the scientist will accomplish more by trying to rest on the Sabbath than if he tries to utilize every day of the week for his professional work. I would counsel all students, if they can, to arrange their schedules so that they do not study on the Sabbath. If students and other seekers after truth will do this, their minds will be quickened and the infinite Spirit will lead them to the verities they wish to learn. This is because God has hallowed his day and blessed it as a perpetual covenant of faithfulness (see Exodus 31:16).

On February 1, 1980, when the First Presidency announced the consolidated Sunday meeting schedule, the following counsel was given:

> A greater responsibility will be placed upon the individual members and families for properly observing the Sabbath day. More time will be available for personal study of the scriptures and family-centered gospel study.
>
> Other appropriate Sabbath activities, such as strengthening family ties, visiting the sick and homebound, giving service to others, writing personal and family histories, genealogical work, and missionary work, should be carefully planned and carried out.
>
> It is expected that this new schedule of meetings and activities will result in greater spiritual growth for members of the Church.[2]

It is hoped that priesthood leaders and members of the Church will honor the spirit of more family togetherness on Sunday.

Keeping the Sabbath Day Holy

The children of Israel were miraculously sustained in the wilderness for more than forty years. They received manna from heaven daily except on the Sabbath. The manna had to be gathered and used the day it fell, or it became wormy and would stink (see Exodus 16:20–30). But on the sixth day, prior to the Sabbath, twice as much manna fell as on the other days (see verse 5). Because the manna did not fall on the Sabbath day, the children of Israel were instructed by the Lord to gather twice as much on the day before the Sabbath so that the food would last for two days. When they did this, a third miracle happened. On the Sabbath day, the manna gathered the day before did not stink, and there were no worms in it, for it was preserved for Sabbath day use (see Exodus 16:24).

Over the centuries, other stories of miraculous happenings relating to Sabbath day observance have been preserved. One is the story of the cobbler working under one of the megalithic stones in Avebury, near Stonehenge, England:

"'One Sunday,' wrote John Saunders in his journal for August 13, 1712, 'a cobler was mending of shoos under one of these great stones. The minute he rose the stone fell down and broke in pieces on the very ground where he sat which made him see the great providence of God in preserving him alive and so deter him from braking the Sabbath for which reason he never more worked on the Sabbath day.'"[3]

A more recent miracle occurred some years ago at the Wells Stake Welfare Tannery, where hides of animals were tanned into leather. On regular work days, the hides were removed from the vats and fresh lime placed in the vats, after which the hides were returned to the lime solution. If the hides were not turned on holidays, they would spoil. But the change was never made on Sunday, and there were no spoiled hides on Monday. Explained J. Lowell Fox, the supervisor of the tannery at the time:

"This brought a strange fact to our minds: holidays are determined by man, and on these days just as on every week day, the hides need to have special care every twelve hours. Sunday is the day

"BRING UP YOUR CHILDREN IN LIGHT AND TRUTH"

set aside by the Lord as a day of rest, and He makes it possible for us to rest from our labors as He has commanded. The hides at the tannery never spoil on Sundays. This is a modern-day miracle, a miracle that happens every weekend!"[4]

Why has God asked us to honor the Sabbath day? The reasons, I think, are at least threefold. The first has to do with the physical need for rest and renewing. Obviously God, who created us, would know more than we do of the limits of our physical and nervous energy and strength.

The second reason is, in my opinion, of far greater significance. It has to do with the need for regeneration and the strengthening of our spiritual being. God knows that left completely to our own devices without regular reminders of our spiritual needs, many of us would degenerate into a preoccupation with satisfying earthly desires and appetites. This need for physical, mental, and spiritual regeneration is met in large measure by faithful observance of the Sabbath day.

The third reason may be the most important of the three. It has to do with obedience to commandments as an expression of our love for God. Blessed are those who need no reasons other than their love for the Savior to keep his commandments. The response of Adam to the angel who asked Adam why he made a sacrifice unto the Lord is a model for all. Responded Adam, "I know not, save the Lord commanded me" (Moses 5:6).

The prophet Samuel reminds us, "To obey is better than sacrifice, and to hearken than the fat of rams" (1 Samuel 15:22).

In this day of increasing access to and preoccupation with materialism, there is a sure protection for ourselves and our children against the plagues of our day. The key to that sure protection surprisingly can be found in Sabbath observance: "And that thou mayest more fully keep thyself unspotted from the world, thou shalt go to the house of prayer and offer up thy sacraments upon my holy day" (D&C 59:9).

Who can question but that sincere Sabbath observance will

Keeping the Sabbath Day Holy

help us keep ourselves unspotted from the world? The injunction to keep the Sabbath day holy is a continuing covenant between God and his elect. The Lord told Moses and the children of Israel: "Verily my sabbaths ye shall keep: for it is a sign between me and you throughout your generations . . . for a perpetual covenant.

"It is a sign between me and the children of Israel forever" (Exodus 31:13, 16–17).

The Mosaic injunctions of Sabbath day observance contained many detailed dos and don'ts. This may have been necessary to teach obedience to those who had been in captivity and had long been denied individual freedom of choice. Thereafter, these Mosaic instructions were carried to many unwarranted extremes that the Savior condemned. In that day the technicalities of Sabbath day observance outweighed the "weightier matters of the law" (Matthew 23:23) such as faith, charity, and the gifts of the Spirit.

In our time God has recognized our intelligence by not requiring endless restrictions. Perhaps this was done with a hope that we would catch more of the spirit of Sabbath worship rather than the letter thereof. In our day, however, the pendulum of Sabbath day desecration has swung very far indeed. We stand in jeopardy of losing great promised blessings. After all, obedience to the covenants of the gospel is a test by which the Lord seeks to "prove you in all things" (D&C 98:14) to see if your devotion is complete.

Where is the line as to what is acceptable and unacceptable on the Sabbath? Within the guidelines, each of us must answer this question for ourselves. While these guidelines are contained in the scriptures and in the words of the modern prophets, they must also be written in our hearts and governed by our consciences. Brigham Young said of the faithful that "The spirit of their religion leaks out of their hearts."[5] It is quite unlikely that there will be any serious violation of Sabbath worship if we come humbly before the Lord and offer him all our heart, our soul, and our mind (see Matthew 22:37).

On the Sabbath day we should do what we have to do and

"Bring Up Your Children in Light and Truth"

what we ought to do in an attitude of worshipfulness and then limit our other activities. We will gain the blessings of Sabbath day worship if we thus honor the Sabbath "with singleness of heart" (D&C 59:13), for the Lord himself has promised us that "he who doeth the works of righteousness shall receive his reward, even peace in this world, and eternal life in the world to come" (verse 23). I encourage us all to regain the peace of the Sabbath by honoring the Lord's day and keeping it holy.

NOTES

1. *The Miracle of Forgiveness* (Salt Lake City: Bookcraft, 1969), pp. 96–97.

2. "Meeting Schedule Approved," *Church News*, 2 Feb. 1980, p. 3.

3. Michael Pitts, *Footprints through Avebury* (Dorchester, England: The Friary Press Limited, 1985), pp. 31–32.

4. *Handbook for Guide Patrol Leaders* (Salt Lake City: The Church of Jesus Christ of Latter-day Saints, 1964), p. 37.

5. In *Journal of Discourses*, 15:83.

CHAPTER FOURTEEN

Magnifying the Priesthood

T HE OBJECT OF God's work is "to bring to pass the immortality and eternal life of man" (Moses 1:39). At various times since Adam's day, God has given the priesthood to man in order to bring about the great plan of salvation for all mankind. Through our faithfulness, the transcendent blessings of eternal life flow from this priesthood authority.

For these priesthood blessings to flower, there is a constant need for unity within the priesthood. We must be loyal to the leaders who have been called to preside over us and hold the keys of the priesthood. The words of President J. Reuben Clark Jr. still ring loudly in our ears: "*Brethren, let us be united.*" He explained: "An essential part of unity is loyalty. . . . Loyalty is a pretty difficult quality to possess. It requires the ability to put away selfishness, greed, ambition and all of the baser qualities of the human mind. You cannot be loyal unless you are willing to surrender. . . . [A person's] own preferences and desires must be put away, and he must see only the great purpose which lies out ahead."[1]

What is the nature of the priesthood? President Brigham Young said of the priesthood, "It is the law by which the worlds are, were, and will continue for ever and ever. It is that system which brings worlds into existence and peoples them, gives them their revolutions—their days, weeks, months, years, their seasons and times."[2] The Prophet Joseph taught that the priesthood's "institution was prior to 'the foundation of this earth, or the morning stars sang together, or the Sons of God shouted for joy,' and is the highest and holiest Priesthood, and is after the order of the Son of God."[3] There is no question that the power of the priesthood exceeds our understanding. Through the Prophet Joseph, the Lord taught "that every one being ordained after this order and calling should have power, by faith, to break mountains, to divide the seas, to dry up waters, to turn them out of their course;

"To put at defiance the armies of nations, to divide the earth, to break every band, to stand in the presence of God; . . . and this by the will of the Son of God which was from before the foundation of the world" (Joseph Smith Translation, Genesis 14:30–31).

The priesthood operates in a system of sublime order. The priesthood is not, however, a floating essence. It must be conferred by ordination with specific offices. It is held by men under sacred duty to use its authority to accomplish God's work for the blessing of men, women, and children alike. No one can claim priesthood authority "except he be ordained by some one who has authority, and it is known to the church that he has authority and has been regularly ordained by the heads of the church" (D&C 42:11). The exercise of priesthood authority is directed by the keys of the priesthood. These keys rest with the presiding local and General Authorities of the Church. Those who have the keys are responsible for the guiding momentum and direction of the work of the Lord on the earth. Clearly, as Alma states, the shepherds of the Church are responsible for protecting the flock:

"For what shepherd is there among you having many sheep doth not watch over them, that the wolves enter not and devour his flock? And behold, if a wolf enter his flock doth he not drive him out?" (Alma 5:59).

Those who have keys, which include the judicial or disciplinary authority, have the responsibility for keeping the Church cleansed from all iniquity (see D&C 20:54; 43:11). Bishops, stake presidents, mission presidents, and others who have the responsibility of keeping the Church pure must perform this labor in a spirit of love and kindness. It should not be done in a spirit of punishment but rather of helping. However, it is of no kindness to a brother or sister in transgression for their presiding officers to look the other way. Some words on this subject come from President John Taylor:

> Furthermore, I have heard of some Bishops who have been seeking to cover up the iniquities of men; I tell them, in the name of God, they will have to bear . . . that iniquity, and if any of you want to partake of the sins of men, or uphold them, you will have to bear them. Do you hear it, you Bishops and you Presidents? God will require it at your hands. You are not placed in [a] position to tamper with the principles of righteousness, nor to cover up the infamies and corruptions of men.[4]

On this matter we urge you presiding brethren to seek the Spirit of God, to study and be guided by the scriptures and the *General Handbook of Instructions.* Church discipline is not limited to sexual sins but includes other acts such as murder, abortion, burglary, theft, fraud and other dishonesty, deliberate disobedience to the rules and regulations of the Church, advocating or practicing polygamy, apostasy, or any other unchristian conduct, including defiance or ridicule of the Lord's anointed contrary to the law of the Lord and the order of the Church.

How does the priesthood function? The decisions of the leaders and quorums of the priesthood should follow the pattern of the presiding quorums. "The decisions of these quorums . . . are to be made in all righteousness, in holiness, and lowliness of heart, meekness and long suffering, and in faith, and virtue, and knowledge, temperance, patience, godliness, brotherly kindness and charity" (D&C 107:30).

In some legislative assemblies of the world, there are some groups termed the "loyal opposition." I find no such principle in the gospel of Jesus Christ; opposition to the word of God cannot be

"Bring Up Your Children in Light and Truth"

loyal. The Savior gave us this solemn warning: "Be one; and if ye are not one ye are not mine" (D&C 38:27). The Lord made it clear that in the presiding quorums, every decision "must be by the unanimous voice of the same; that is, every member in each quorum must be agreed to its decisions" (D&C 107:27). This means that after frank and open discussion, decisions are reached in council under the direction of the presiding officer, who has the ultimate authority to decide. That decision is then sustained, because our unity comes from full agreement with righteous principles and also from our general response to the operation of the Spirit of God.

Free discussion and expression are encouraged in the Church. Certainly the open expressions in most fast and testimony meetings or Sunday School, Relief Society, and priesthood meetings attest to that principle. However, the privilege of free expression should operate within limits. In 1869, George Q. Cannon explained the limits of individual expression:

> A friend . . . wished to know whether we . . . considered an honest difference of opinion between a member of the Church and the Authorities of the Church was apostasy. . . . We replied that . . . we could conceive of a man honestly differing in opinion from the Authorities of the Church and yet not be an apostate; but we could not conceive of a man publishing these differences of opinion and seeking by arguments, sophistry and special pleading to enforce them upon the people to produce division and strife and to place the acts and counsels of the Authorities of the Church, if possible, in a wrong light, and not be an apostate, for such conduct was apostasy as we understood the term.[5]

Among the activities considered apostate to the Church are instances in which members "(1) repeatedly act in clear, open, and deliberate public opposition to the Church or its leaders; (2) persist in teaching as Church doctrine information that is not Church doctrine after being corrected by their bishops or higher authority; or (3) continue to follow the teachings of apostate cults (such as those that advocate plural marriage) after being corrected by their bishops or higher authority."[6]

Those men and women who persist in publicly challenging basic doctrines, practices, and establishments of the Church sever themselves from the Spirit of the Lord and forfeit their right to place and influence in the Church. Members are encouraged to study the principles and the doctrines of the Church so that they understand them. Then if questions arise and there are honest differences of opinion, members are encouraged to discuss these matters privately with priesthood leaders.

There is a certain arrogance in thinking that any of us may be more spiritually intelligent, more learned, or more righteous than the councils called to preside over us. Those councils are more in tune with the Lord than any individual person they preside over, and the individual members of the councils are generally guided by those councils.

In this church, where we have lay leadership, it is inevitable that some will be placed in authority over us who have a different background from our own. This does not mean that those with other honorable vocational or professional qualifications are any less entitled to the spirit of their office than any other. Some of the great bishops of my lifetime include a brickmason, a grocer, a farmer, a dairyman, and one who ran an ice cream business. What any may have lacked in formal education was insignificant. They were humble men, and because they were humble they were taught and magnified by the Holy Spirit. Without exception they were greatly strengthened as they learned to labor diligently to fulfill their callings and to minister to the Saints they were called to preside over. So it is with all of the callings in the Church. President Thomas S. Monson teaches us, "Whom the Lord calls, the Lord qualifies."[7]

How should holders of the priesthood treat the women of the Church? The sisters of this church since the beginning have always made a great and marvelous contribution to the work of the Lord.

They have added so very much of intelligence, work, culture, and refinement to the Church and our families. The contributions of the sisters as we move into the future are needed more than ever to help establish the values, the faith, and the future success of our families and the well-being of our society. The sisters of the Church need to know they are valued, honored, and appreciated. The sisters who serve as leaders need to be invited to participate and to be listened to and included in our stake and ward council meetings, particularly concerning those matters involving sisters, youth, and children.

How should those who bear the priesthood treat their wives and the other women in their families? Our wives need to be cherished. They need to hear their husbands call them blessed, and the children need to hear their fathers generously praise their mothers (see Proverbs 31:28). The Lord values his daughters just as much as he does his sons. In marriage, neither is superior; each has a different primary and divine responsibility. Chief among these responsibilities for wives is the calling of motherhood. I firmly believe that our dear, faithful sisters enjoy a special spiritual enrichment that is inherent in their natures.

President Spencer W. Kimball states: "To be a righteous woman during the winding up scenes on this earth, before the second coming of our Savior, is an especially noble calling. . . . Other institutions in society may falter and even fail, but the righteous woman can help to save the home, which may be the last and only sanctuary some mortals know in the midst of storm and strife."[8]

Priesthood is a righteous authority only. Any attempt to use it in the home as a club to abuse others or enforce unrighteous dominion is a complete contradiction of that authority and results in its loss. As a holder of the priesthood, the father holds a primary responsibility to claim spiritual and temporal blessings from the Lord for himself, his wife, and his family, but these blessings can be claimed only in righteousness as he honors his priesthood. We are taught by the Lord that "no power or influence can or ought to be maintained by virtue of the priesthood, only by persuasion, by long-suffering, by gentleness and meekness, and by love unfeigned" (D&C 121:41). In my opinion, there are few words in the holy scriptures of greater significance than the beautiful language contained in section 121 of the Doctrine and Covenants as to how the priesthood is to be exercised:

> By kindness, and pure knowledge, which shall greatly enlarge the soul without hypocrisy, and without guile—
> Reproving betimes with sharpness, when moved upon by the Holy Ghost; and then showing forth afterwards an increase of love toward him whom thou hast reproved, lest he esteem thee to be his enemy;
> That he may know that thy faithfulness is stronger than the cords of death.
> Let thy bowels also be full of charity towards all men, and to the household of faith, and let virtue garnish thy thoughts unceasingly; then shall thy confidence wax strong in the presence of God; and the doctrine of the priesthood shall distil upon thy soul as the dews from heaven.
> The Holy Ghost shall be thy constant companion, and thy scepter an unchanging scepter of righteousness and truth; and thy dominion shall be an everlasting dominion, and without compulsory means it shall flow unto thee forever and ever. (D&C 121:42–46)

President Spencer W. Kimball stated, with respect to priesthood covenants: "There is no limit to the power of the priesthood which you hold. The limit comes in you if you do not live in harmony with the Spirit of the Lord and you limit yourselves in the power you exert."[9] President Kimball further stated: "One breaks the priesthood covenant by transgressing commandments—but also by leaving undone his duties. Accordingly, to break this covenant one needs only to do nothing."[10]

Another great reminder of our obligations and blessings is the oath and covenant of the priesthood contained in section 84 of the Doctrine and Covenants. We are told that the transcendent

"BRING UP YOUR CHILDREN IN LIGHT AND TRUTH"

obligations of priesthood holders are "to give diligent heed to the words of eternal life," to bear "testimony to all the world," and to teach the world of the "judgment which is to come" (verses 43, 61, 87). Then there is this marvelous promise if we are faithful in our priesthood responsibilities: we shall be "sanctified by the Spirit" and become "the elect of God," and "all that [the] Father hath shall be given unto him" (verses 33–34, 38). How much more important it is to receive "all that [the] Father hath" than to seek or receive anything else this life offers.

The crowning blessings of life come through obeying the covenants and honoring the ordinances received in the holy temples, including the new and everlasting covenant of marriage, which is the capstone of the holy endowment.

In our desire to be broad-minded, to be accepted, to be liked and admired, let us not trifle with the doctrines and the covenants that have been revealed to us nor with the pronouncements of those who have been given the keys of the kingdom of God on earth. For all of us, the words of Joshua ring with increasing relevance: "Choose you this day whom ye will serve; . . . but as for me and my house, we will serve the Lord" (Joshua 24:15).

NOTES

1. *Immortality and Eternal Life,* Melchizedek Priesthood course of study, 1968–69 (Salt Lake City: The Church of Jesus Christ of Latter-day Saints, 1967), p. 163.

2. *Discourses of Brigham Young,* sel. John A. Widtsoe (Salt Lake City: Deseret Book Co., 1977), p. 130.

3. *Teachings of the Prophet Joseph Smith,* p. 167.

4. In Conference Report, April 1880, p. 78.

5. *Gospel Truth,* sel. Jerreld L. Newquist, 2 vols. (Salt Lake City: Deseret Book Co., 1974), 2:276–77.

6. *General Handbook of Instructions,* 1989, p. 10-3.

7. In Conference Report, April 1988, p. 52; or *Ensign,* May 1988, p. 43.

8. *Ensign,* November 1978, p. 103.

9. *The Teachings of Spencer W. Kimball,* ed. Edward L. Kimball (Salt Lake City: Bookcraft, 1982), p. 498.

10. *The Teachings of Spencer W. Kimball,* p. 497.

CHAPTER FIFTEEN

Priesthood Holders as Shepherds

ELDER BRUCE R. MCCONKIE stated: "Anyone serving in any capacity in the Church in which he is responsible for the spiritual or temporal well-being of any of the Lord's children is a shepherd to those sheep. The Lord holds his shepherds accountable for the safety [meaning the salvation] of his sheep."[1] The bearers of the priesthood have this great responsibility, whether they serve as father, grandfather, home teacher, elders quorum president, bishop, stake president, or in another Church calling.

Initially, let us consider the worthy young men of the Aaronic Priesthood. When I was a very small boy, my father found a lamb all alone out in the desert. The herd of sheep to which its mother belonged had moved on, and somehow the lamb got separated from its mother, and the shepherd must not have known that the lamb was lost. Because it could not survive alone in the desert, my father picked it up and brought it home. To have left the lamb there would have meant certain death, either by falling prey to the coyotes or by starvation because it was so young that it still needed milk. Some sheepherders call these lambs "bummers." My father gave the lamb to me and I became its shepherd.

For several weeks I warmed cow's milk in a baby's bottle and fed the lamb. We became fast friends. I called him Nigh (I don't remember where I got the name). It began to grow. My lamb and I would play on the lawn. Sometimes we would lie together on the grass and I would lay my head on its soft, woolly side and look up at the blue sky and the white, billowing clouds. I did not lock my lamb up during the day. It would not run away. It soon learned to eat grass. I could call my lamb from anywhere in the yard by just imitating as best I could the bleating sound of a sheep: *Baa. Baa.*

One night there came a terrible storm. I forgot to put my lamb in the barn that night as I should have done. I went to bed. My little friend was frightened in the storm, and I could hear it bleating. I knew that I should help my pet, but I wanted to stay safe, warm, and dry in my bed. I didn't get up as I should have done. The next morning I went out to find my lamb dead. A dog had also heard its bleating cry and killed it. My heart was broken. I had not been a good shepherd or steward of that which my father had entrusted to me. My father said, "Son, couldn't I trust you to take care of just one lamb?" My father's remark hurt me even more than losing my woolly friend. I resolved that day, as a little boy, that I would try never again to neglect my stewardship as a shepherd if I was ever placed in that position again.

Not too many years thereafter I was called as a junior companion to a home teacher. There were times when it was so cold or stormy that I wanted to stay home and be comfortable, but in my mind's ear I could hear my little lamb bleating, and I knew I needed to be a good shepherd and go with my senior companion. In all the many intervening years, whenever I have had a desire to shirk my duties, there has come to me a remembrance of how sorry I was that night so many years ago when I had not been a good shepherd. I have not always done everything I should have, but I have tried.

I should like to speak for a few minutes about the constitutional duties of the Lord's shepherds. By that I mean those responsibilities that are contained in the revelations given by the Lord himself. There is no greater responsibility than that of being a husband and a father, from which there is no release. The Lord said, "Thou shalt love thy wife with all thy heart, and shalt cleave unto her and none else" (D&C 42:22). The Lord further says to the fathers of this church, "I have commanded you to bring up your children in light and truth" (D&C 93:40).

"And they shall also teach their children to pray, and to walk uprightly before the Lord.

"And the inhabitants of Zion shall also observe the Sabbath day to keep it holy" (D&C 68:28–29).

Another great responsibility is that of the home teacher. "The teacher's duty is to watch over the church always, and be with and strengthen them;

"And see that there is no iniquity in the church, neither hardness with each other, neither lying, backbiting, nor evil speaking" (D&C 20:53–54). A further commandment is to "see that the church meet together often, and also see that all the members do their duty" (verse 55). They are to "warn, expound, exhort, and teach, and invite all to come unto Christ" (verse 59).

The priesthood quorum presidents and their counselors are also shepherds of the sheepfold and bear the responsibility to lovingly care for the members of their quorums. The bishops of the Church are some of the watchmen on the tower. Said Timothy to the bishops of the Church:

> This is a true saying, If a man desire the office of a bishop, he desireth a good work.
>
> A bishop then must be blameless, the husband of one wife, vigilant, sober, of good behaviour, given to hospitality, apt to teach;
>
> Not given to wine, no striker, not greedy of filthy lucre; but patient, not a brawler, not covetous;
>
> One that ruleth well his own house, having his children in subjection with all gravity;
>
> (For if a man know not how to rule his own house, how shall he take care of the church of God?)(1 Timothy 3:1–5)

Of the Aaronic Priesthood the Lord has said, "The bishopric is the presidency of this priesthood, and holds the keys or authority of the same" (D&C 107:15). Bishops, our young men are experiencing the storms of life. There are vicious wolves prowling to devour them. Many of them are like my little lamb, crying out for help. We plead with you bishops to do all you can to keep them safe.

The stake president is also a constitutional officer of the Church, for he presides over the stake, which the Lord has said "may be for a defense, and for a refuge from the storm, and from wrath when it shall be poured out without mixture upon the whole earth" (D&C 115:6). The stakes are "the curtains or the strength of Zion" (D&C 101:21). They are to be spiritual centers of righteousness, strength, and protection.

The Presiding Bishopric, each of whom is an ordained bishop, have the responsibility for directing the temporal affairs of the Church as assigned by the First Presidency. In this great worldwide Church, the responsibility of the Presiding Bishopric is heavy and great.

The Lord said of the Seventy:

> The Seventy are also called to preach the gospel, and to be especial witnesses unto the Gentiles and in all the world—thus differing from other officers in the church in the duties of their calling. . . .
>
> The Seventy are to act in the name of the Lord, under the direction of the Twelve or the traveling high council, in building up the church and regulating all the affairs of the same in all nations, first unto the Gentiles and then to the Jews. (D&C 107:25, 34)

The Twelve Apostles are the "special witnesses of the name of Christ in all the world, thus differing from other officers in the church in the duties of their calling" (verse 23). The Lord said they are "being sent out, holding the keys, to open the door by the proclamation of the gospel of Jesus Christ" (verse 35). The Twelve are the legates of the Lord.

The First Presidency have the ultimate responsibility for the affairs of the kingdom of God on the earth. Of them the Lord has said:

> Of the Melchizedek Priesthood, three Presiding High Priests, chosen by the body, appointed and ordained to that office, and upheld by the confidence, faith, and prayer of the church, form a quorum of the Presidency of the Church. . . .
>
> And the Presidency of the council of the High Priesthood shall have power to call other high priests, even twelve, to assist as counselors; and thus the Presidency of the High Priesthood and its counselors shall have power to decide upon testimony according to the laws of the church. (Verses 22, 79)

Of the President of the Church, the Lord has said that he is the "President of the High Priesthood of the Church;

"Or, in other words, the Presiding High Priest over the High Priesthood of the Church" (verses 65–66). He is "to preside over the whole church, and to be like unto Moses— . . . to be a seer, a revelator, a translator, and a prophet, having all the gifts of God which he bestows upon the head of the church" (verses 91–92; see D&C 21:1).

The President of the Church directs the use of all of the keys and authority of the priesthood and is the only person who can exercise all of them, even though all of the ordained Apostles hold these keys, some of which are in latent form.

Brethren, I have been a member of the First Presidency for a relatively short time. It seems as though before I had this calling I had limited vision, but I have now put on glasses that allow me to see more clearly, in a small way, the magnitude of the responsibility of the President of the Church. I am afraid I am like the aristocrat who wore a monocle in one eye. Of him it was said, "He could see more than he could comprehend." The men who see most clearly the big picture are these giants of the Lord, President Gordon B. Hinckley and President Thomas S. Monson, who have served many years faithfully as counselors to the previous Presidents of the Church.

"Bring Up Your Children in Light and Truth"

In a church as vast and far-reaching as ours, there must be order. We must have, in addition to the scriptures and modern revelations, guidelines and procedures for the Church to move forward around the world in an orderly manner. There are some elements of bureaucracy that cannot help but occasionally produce some irritation and perhaps frustration. We ask you to look beyond any irritations or inconvenience in Church administration. We ask you to focus and concentrate on the simple, sublime, spiritually nourishing, and saving principles of the gospel. We ask you to stand steady. We ask you to be faithful in your stewardships as the shepherding priesthood authority of the Church. Let us be true to our callings and the holy priesthood we bear. Let us be united in supporting and sustaining those in authority over us.

Brethren, after more than sixty years, I can still hear in my mind the bleating, frightened cry of the lamb of my boyhood that I did not shepherd as I should have. I can also remember the loving rebuke of my father: "Son, couldn't I trust you to take care of just one lamb?" If we are not good shepherds, I wonder how we will feel in the eternities.

> Jesus saith to Simon Peter, Simon, son of Jonas, lovest thou me more than these? He saith unto him, Yea, Lord; thou knowest that I love thee. He saith unto him, Feed my lambs.
>
> He saith to him again the second time, Simon, son of Jonas, lovest thou me? He saith unto him, Yea, Lord; thou knowest that I love thee. He saith unto him, Feed my sheep.
>
> He saith unto him the third time, Simon, son of Jonas, lovest thou me? Peter was grieved because he said unto him the third time, Lovest thou me? And he said unto him, Lord, thou knowest all things; thou knowest that I love thee. Jesus saith unto him, Feed my sheep. (John 21:15–17)

NOTE

1. *Mormon Doctrine,* 2d ed. (Salt Lake City: Bookcraft, 1966), p. 710.

CHAPTER SIXTEEN

Fathers, Mothers, Marriage

In RECENT TIMES, society has been plagued with a cancer from which few families have escaped. I speak of the disintegration of our homes. Immediate corrective treatment is urgent. I affirm my profound belief that God's greatest creation is womanhood. I also believe that there is no greater good in all the world than motherhood. The influence of a mother in the lives of her children is beyond calculation. Single parents, most of whom are mothers, perform an especially heroic service.

I hasten to acknowledge that there are too many husbands and fathers who are abusive to their wives and children and from whom the wives and children need protection. Yet modern sociological studies powerfully reaffirm the essential influence of a caring father in the life of a child—boy or girl. In the past twenty years, as homes and families have struggled to stay intact, sociological studies reveal this alarming fact: much of the crime and many of the behavioral disorders in the United States come from homes where the father has abandoned the children. In many societies the world over, child poverty, crime, drug abuse, and family decay can be traced to conditions where the father gives no male nurturing. Sociologically it is now painfully apparent that fathers are not optional family baggage.

We need to honor the position of the father as the primary provider for physical and spiritual support. I state this with no reluctance, because the Lord has revealed that this obligation is placed upon husbands. "Women have claim on their husbands for their maintenance, until their husbands are taken" (D&C 83:2). Further, "all children have claim upon their parents for their maintenance until they are of age" (D&C 83:4). In addition, their spiritual welfare should be "brought to pass by the faith and covenant of their fathers" (D&C 84:99). As regards little children, the Lord has promised that "great things may be required at the hand of their fathers" (D&C 29:48).

It is useless to debate which parent is most important. No one would doubt that a mother's influence is paramount with newborns and in the first years of a child's life. The father's influence increases as the child grows older. However, each parent is necessary at various times in a child's development. Both fathers and mothers do many intrinsically different things for their children. Both mothers and fathers are equipped to nurture children, but their approaches are different. Mothers seem to take a dominant role in preparing children to live within their families, present and future. Fathers seem best equipped to prepare children to function in the environment outside the family.

One authority states: "Studies show that fathers have a special role to play in building a child's self-respect. They are important, too, in ways we really don't understand, in developing internal limits and controls in children." He continues: "Research also shows that fathers are critical in establishment of gender in children. Interestingly, fatherly involvement produces stronger sexual identity and character in both boys and girls. It is well established that the masculinity of sons and the femininity of daughters are each greater when fathers are active in family life."[1]

Parents in any marital situation have a duty to set aside personal differences and encourage each other's righteous influence in the lives of their children.

Is it not possible to give to womankind all the rights and blessings that come from God and legal authority without diminishing the nobility of God's other grand creation, manhood? Eliza R. Snow stated in 1872:

> The status of women is one of the questions of the day. Socially and politically it forces itself upon the attention of the world. Some . . . refuse to concede that woman is entitled to the enjoyment of any rights other than . . . the whims, fancies or justice . . . men may choose to grant her. The reasons which they cannot meet with argument they decry and ridicule; an old refuge for those opposed to correct principles which they are unable to controvert. Others . . . not only recognize that woman's status should be improved, but are so radical in their extreme theories that they would set her in antagonism to man, assume for her a separate and opposing existence; and . . . show how entirely independent she should be. [Indeed, they] would make her adopt the more reprehensible phases of character which men present, and which should be shunned or improved by them instead of being copied by women. These are the two extremes, and between them is the "golden mean."[2]

Many people do not understand our belief that God has wisely established a guiding authority for the most important institutions in the world. This guiding authority is called the priesthood. The priesthood is held in trust to be used to bless all of God's children. Priesthood is not gender; it is blessings from God for all at the hands of the servants he has designated. Within the Church this authority of the priesthood can bless all members through the ministration of home teachers, quorum presidents, bishops, fathers, and all other righteous brethren who are charged with the administration of the affairs of the kingdom of God. Priesthood is the righteous power and influence by which boys are taught in their youth and throughout their lives to honor chastity, to be honest and industrious, and to develop respect for and stand in the defense of womanhood. Priesthood is a restraining influence. Girls are taught that through its influence and power to bless, they can fulfill many of their desires.

Holding the priesthood means following the example of Christ and seeking to emulate his example of fatherhood. It means constant concern and caring for one's own flesh and blood. The man who holds the priesthood is to honor it by eternally cherishing, with absolute fidelity, his wife and the mother of his children. He is to extend lifelong care and concern for his children and their children. The plea of David for his rebel son is one of the most moving in all of the scriptures: "O my son Absalom, my son, my son Absalom! would God I had died for thee, O Absalom, my son, my son!" (2 Samuel 18:33).

I urge each husband and father of this church to be the kind of a man your wife would not want to be without. I urge the sisters of this church to be patient, loving, and understanding with their husbands. Those who enter into marriage should be fully prepared to establish their marriage as the first priority in their lives.

It is destructive to the feeling essential for a happy marriage for either party to say to the other marriage partner, "I don't need you." This is particularly so because the counsel of the Savior was and is to become one flesh: "For this cause shall a man leave father and mother, and shall cleave to his wife: and they twain shall be one flesh. Wherefore they are no more twain, but one flesh" (Matthew 19:5–6).

It is far more difficult to be of one heart and mind than to be physically one. This unity of heart and mind is manifest in sincere expressions of "I appreciate you" and "I am proud of you." Such domestic harmony results from forgiving and forgetting, essential elements of a maturing marriage relationship. Someone has said that we should keep our eyes wide open before marriage and half shut afterward.[3] True charity ought to begin in marriage, for it is a relationship that must be rebuilt every day.

I wonder if it is possible for one marriage partner to jettison the other and become completely whole. Either partner who diminishes the divine role of the other in the presence of the children demeans the budding femininity within the daughters and the

Fathers, Mothers, Marriage

emerging manhood of the sons. I suppose there are always some honest differences between husband and wife, but let them be settled in private.

The importance of this subject emboldens me to say a word about covenant breaking. It must be recognized that some marriages just fail. To those in that circumstance, I extend understanding, and I recognize that every divorce carries heartache with it. I hope what I say will not be disturbing. In my opinion, any promise between a man and a woman incident to a marriage ceremony rises to the dignity of a covenant. The family relationship of father, mother, and child is the oldest and most enduring institution in the world. It has survived vast differences of geography and culture. This is because marriage between man and woman is a natural state and is ordained of God. It is a moral imperative. Those marriages performed in our temples, then, meant to be eternal relationships, become the most sacred covenants we can make. The sealing power given by God through Elijah is thus invoked, and God becomes a party to the promises.

What, then, might be "just cause" for breaking the covenants of marriage? Over a lifetime of dealing with human problems, I have struggled to understand what might be considered "just cause" for breaking of marriage covenants. I confess I do not claim the wisdom or authority to definitively state what is "just cause." Only the parties to the marriage can determine this. They must bear the responsibility for the train of consequences that inevitably follows if these covenants are not honored. In my opinion, "just cause" should be nothing less serious than a prolonged and apparently irredeemable relationship that is destructive of a person's dignity as a human being.

At the same time, I have strong feelings about what is not provocation for breaking the sacred covenants of marriage. Surely it is not simply "mental distress" or "personality differences" or having "grown apart" or having "fallen out of love." This is especially so where there are children. Enduring divine counsel comes from Paul:

"Husbands, love your wives, even as Christ also loved the church, and gave himself for it" (Ephesians 5:25).

"That they may teach the young women to be sober, to love their husbands, [and] to love their children" (Titus 2:4).

In my opinion, members of the Church have the most effective cure for our decaying family life. That cure is for men, women, and children to honor and respect the divine roles of both fathers and mothers in the home. In so doing, mutual respect and appreciation among the members of the Church will be fostered by the righteousness found there. In this way the great sealing keys restored by Elijah and spoken of by Malachi might operate "to turn the hearts of the fathers to the children, and the children to the fathers, lest the whole earth be smitten with a curse" (D&C 110:15; see Malachi 4:6).

President Joseph Fielding Smith stated concerning the keys of Elijah: "This sealing power bestowed upon Elijah, is the power which binds husbands and wives, and children to parents for time and eternity. It is the binding power existing in every Gospel ordinance. . . . It was the mission Elijah to come, and restore it so that the curse of confusion and disorder would not exist in the kingdom of God."[4] Confusion and disorder are all too common in society, but they must not be permitted to destroy our homes.

Perhaps we regard the power bestowed by Elijah as something associated only with formal ordinances performed in sacred places. But these ordinances become dynamic and productive of good only as they reveal themselves in our daily lives. Malachi said that the power of Elijah would turn the *hearts* of the fathers and the children to each other (see Malachi 4:5–6). The heart is the seat of the emotions and a conduit for revelation. This sealing power thus reveals itself in family relationships, in attributes and virtues developed in a nurturing environment and in loving service. These are the cords that bind families together, and the priesthood advances their development. In imperceptible but real ways, the "doctrine of the priesthood shall distil upon thy soul [and thy home] as the dews from heaven" (D&C 121:45).

I testify that the blessings of the priesthood, honored by fathers and husbands and revered by wives and children, can indeed cure the cancer that plagues our society. I plead with you, fathers, come home. Magnify your priesthood calling; bless your families through this sacred influence, and experience the rewards promised by our Father and God.

NOTES

1. Karl Zinsmeister, "Do Children Need Fathers?" *Crisis,* October 1992.

2. "Woman's Status," *The Woman's Exponent,* 15 July 1872, p. 29.

3. Magdeleine de Scudéry, in John P. Bradley et al., comp., *The International Dictionary of Thoughts* (Chicago: J. G. Ferguson Publishing Co., 1969), p. 472.

4. *Elijah the Prophet and His Mission* (Salt Lake City: Deseret Book Co., 1957), p. 5.

Index

INDEX

INDEX

INDEX

INDEX